THE MAN
AT THE
TABLE

Charleston, SC
www.PalmettoPublishing.com

The Man At The Table
Copyright © 2023 by Gary Kinsey
Copyright by Tree City Labs, 2023

Hardcover ISBN: 979-8-8229-2475-8
Paperback ISBN: 979-8-8229-2476-5
eBook ISBN: 979-8-8229-2477-2

THE MAN
AT THE
TABLE

GARY KINSEY

DISCLAIMER

The author is not a medical doctor, and no parts of the book are intended to serve as official medical advice. All events are true, but most names have been changed to protect their identities.

DEDICATION

To all the weed smugglers and pirates who paved the way through
these treacherous times

THE MAN AT THE TABLE

I was supposed to sell insurance for a living when I moved to Florida.

Instead, I sold drugs. And I smuggled them. And I used them.

Still do. Use, that is. Every fucking day.

In fact, I've made my life's work all about drugs. And you know what? A lot of wisdom has come out of my world of weed.

See, I grew up in a small town in Indiana, where religion ruled everything. I mean everything. The church's ideology, I learned very early, wasn't about freedom. It was about the exact opposite. It was about imposing rules and structure and closing off minds. And that dogma was against every single fiber of my being. I wanted to live my life my way—and help people open their minds, heal their bodies, and find their own spirituality in life in whatever they wanted.

That's living.

So when I got away from that town and found a new life on the beaches of Florida, everything changed.

I lived the druggie, hippie life (oh the women, oh the parties, oh the freedom I felt). And that's the point when I became fascinated with a much more lucrative path—one in which I could sell and smuggle.

Those adventures were ones I experienced that few others could even imagine.

In these pages, I've laid it all out—all of my journey (the literal highs and the rock-bottom lows) and everything I've learned from them. So yeah, in these pages…

- You'll read about the time I smuggled more than five tons of marijuana from Colombia and almost died doing so.
- You'll read about how I got into the dealing business.
- You'll read about the 17-day cocaine bender I went on.
- You'll read about how I changed from being a destructive drunk to being a sober, college-educated physical therapist who after retiring, became an edible-producing entrepreneur.
- And you'll read about how I—now in my mid-70s—have created a local market on nature's best medicine.

I wanted to name this book something else: "Fuck You, Richard Nixon." The phrase comes from something I yelled to the sky at the end of my first big smuggle, but it represents something so much bigger: How much I loathe the government's fucking crackdown on drugs back in the 1970s and how it has systematically prevented people from enjoying the freedoms and powers of marijuana (and more recently, those magic mushrooms). I decided against the Richard Nixon title, because, 1) I probably shouldn't put "fuck" in the title of a book, even though I use that word a whole fucking lot in this book and 2) I had serious doubts whether the people who read this book will even know who the fuck Richard Nixon is. (He was the 37th U.S. President.)

The Man at the Table much better symbolizes the way I've approached business—from the time I started selling drugs to everything I have done since.

I always did business at a table.

Not back alleys, not bar bathrooms, not on the streets.

At the fucking table.

From my first days selling weed on St. Pete Beach, I'd invite people to my place, and we'd sit at the table—and talk. And in just about every house I lived in, I had a table that acted like my central hub—and that's where we'd do business.

See, I had this basic motto: If you can't trust a person enough to invite them into your home and sit at your table and have a conversation, then you shouldn't do business with them. Sit, talk, trust. Frankly, I also wanted to see if you could handle your shit. And if you couldn't handle your shit, then I didn't want to make any deals with you. (For what it's worth, my favorite table was the one I had in my place in Madeira Beach, Florida. It was a beautiful, oblong table that I bought with the house—and I had it at a time in my life where we smoked a lot of weed, did a lot of coke, and drank a fuckload of booze. Back then, my liquor bills were almost $600 a week. Holy fuck, we plowed through some shit.)

But to this day, all my business—and all of the relationships I've built through my business—happened at my table. (Even this book was written at my table.)

In a way, I hope that "The Man at the Table" isn't just about a location, but really symbolizes something more—the stories I've shared, the experiences I've had, the lessons I've learned and tried to share with others, and (I hope) a small nod to the fact that a lot of people have learned to look at me as someone who can help them not only with the products I offer, but also with the wisdom I try to pass along.

After I take you through my journey—starting with the days of country living (and that oppressive religion I endured as a kid) and ending with what I'm doing today, with a middle that involves a whole lot of drugs, a whole lot of sex, and a whole lot of *living*—I'll wrap up with this: The end of the book includes an exploration of the most profound things I've learned in the healing industry. That's right. The healing industry. That's how I think about what I've been part of.

Helping people heal. Helping people open their minds. Helping people take the pain away. Helping people live life fully.

Why is this such an important tale? And why tell it now?

It's an amazing story, or so my clients tell me over and over again when I share pieces of it with them. And I wanted to write this book because I wanted to capture everything—my smuggles, my struggles, and my snuggles (you're going to read a lot about my life of lust, and there really wasn't a whole lot of snuggling going on, but you get the picture). I wanted to share how my experiences in the drug-dealing and edible-making industries reflect some of the universal truths about the world and all of us who are fortunate enough to live in it.

Today, we're at a fascinating point in the history of recreational and medicinal drug use in this country. I've spent my life dealing in the dark, but we're very close to living in a world where the war on recreational drugs has stopped and has turned into an important medicinal and economic part of our world. My hope is that every person has the access, ability, and means to get the help they need.

It's been quite a ride. Hell, some may even call it an incr*edible* journey.

Thank you for coming along on this one with me.

TABLE OF CONTENTS

CHAPTER 1

GRANDPA, I SOLD YOUR BOOK OF NAKED WOMEN

My father, a World War II P51 fighter pilot, got discharged in November 1945. When F.M. (which stood for Francis Merlin) came home, he proposed to his girlfriend, Clara Louise.

"I don't love you," Clara Louise responded.

F.M. simply told her, "Well, you'll learn to."

Clara Louise was 19 at the time, and she grew up as a sickly little girl, an only child. That was unusual because her mother was the oldest child of 14 kids, and she always wore the guilt of the fact that she had to get married because she was pregnant and lived with that shame all of her life. Clara Louise's father was also the first of 14 kids. My dad was born in 1920, and mom in 1926.

My mom and dad both grew up and met in Iowa, and that's where we'd vacation—out at my grandfather's 100-acre farm. Grandpa Kinsey. They lived the old-country farm life out there. Milked the cows, made their own cream, shit like that. Kinda neat when you think about self-reliance and the simple life.

But I tell you, Granpda Kinsey was a hard-core Nazi—racist as hell, and he actually thought Hitler had the right ideas when it came to Jews and blacks (fuck, he even wore Hitler's style moustache). The only thing that man ever gave me in his life was a large swastika flag from Nazi Germany.

F.M. and Clara Louise did get married, they made me, and I was born in August 1946 in Anderson, Indiana.

Anderson—named after a Lenape chief—was a small town about 45 miles outside of Indianapolis. It had about 350 people when it was incorporated back in 1838, and if you ask me, never felt much bigger than that in the century after that, though the population is around 50,000 today. Anderson was an industrial city with car factories (General Motors was big there), but it really was as much of a religious center too. The Church of God of Anderson set up its world headquarters there in 1905, and that's not even counting the seminary that opened there too.

My mom didn't work. She was sick all the time, so sick that she got addicted to valium. My father was addicted to God. Dad worked during the days testing jet engines at a General Motors factory, making 50 bucks a week, and then after dinner, he'd work at my other grandpa's mechanic's garage. Looking back, I think he worked two jobs because he didn't want to do the "father" part of being a father. So he worked two jobs, my mom did all the chores, and we kids helped with everything around the house. Cleaning up, various jobs around the house, stuff like that.

Dad grew up in a religious family, and his whole life revolved around the church. We even went to church twice on Sundays. My dad never drank. Hell, he never did anything he wasn't supposed to (except be hard as hell on me, I suppose), because of his religious upbringing. That's another reason why my mother never worked. Dad thought the man of the house had to provide and that the wife should stay at home. So we struggled.

My parents grew up with hard-core Christianity, and that religion became a huge influence in our life. Anderson, Indiana, was a factory town that put out two things—car parts and preachers. What's funny is that even though my father was as religious as it gets, he always had a judgment about someone else—especially other religions. Every Sunday, we'd drive by the Catholic church, and he'd make the same remark: "They go out every Saturday and drink and screw and then say they're sorry, and then everything's ok."

God, he hated the hypocrisy.

Every Sunday, I'd hear this shit.

Me? I'm thinking what the hell is so wrong with drinking and fucking?

But as it goes, religious was embedded in my DNA, so it wasn't just part of who we were. It *was* who we were. My uncle was a preacher in Lebanon, Indiana. The men of the family dug a hole in the ground and basement for a church for him (and then the church was later built around him). He was great man, and even worked in the local jails counseling prisoners after he retired from the ministry.

Our life revolved around the church. My mom, I suspect, even had a crush on one of the ministers, because he was a piano-playing man and my mom loved piano. (That minister was later caught having affairs, though I don't think my mom ever let him run his fingers along her keys, if you know what I'm saying.)

Anything else we did was always "in between." In between services, because life was defined by when we'd go to church. It was food and church, food and church.

Lots of praying. Lots of meat loaf.

Because of religion, we couldn't do normal things. We weren't allowed to go to sock hops. We couldn't even drink Coca-Cola. Shit like that with no explanation.

Religion was confusing to me, because of one simple fact: Nobody could answer your questions. Nobody could answer, "Why? Why do I have to believe this?"

Well, they said, you've just got to. Because that's the way it is. You have to have faith.

I didn't.

I didn't understand what faith was. I didn't get it. We have this biblical story laid out in front of us, and it didn't explain anything. Just accept it, my parents said. I couldn't, because I'm a logical person and I couldn't get past the whole notion of "you just have to think what you think because that's the way it was." I didn't really start dissecting it until I got to college at Ball State where I took a philosophy class and learned about a lot of religions; as my education and curiosity increased, it helped open up to all sorts of thinking that anything is possible. Descartes was a big influence on me—"I think therefore I am."

Just growing up in that whole religious atmosphere was so morbid. It felt like it was death, death, death, old, old, old. Old fat ladies sat on doughnut-shaped cushions because they had fucking

4

hemorrhoids. Some of them washed their feet in church. Fuuuuck. What is this? Well, they were imitating the bible, and I'm thinking that the bible was a long, long time ago, so what the fuck are we even doing?

I challenged authority my whole life (and I paid the price for it, as you will see), but it really started here as I challenged religion because it didn't make any sense to me.

Soon after my dad returned from war, my mom and dad settled in Indiana. Cold as Fuck, Indiana, if you ask me.

My parents had three daughters after me. Deeann was the oldest, 18 months younger than me. She was an honors student at Ball State and married her high school boyfriend. Vicki was six years younger than me and was the opposite of Deeann's sweet and gentle personality. And Christina was four years younger than Vicki, and she turned out to be the best one out of all of us—ended up being my mother's caregiver when she got sick in her late years.

My dad was a hero. Not my hero, but he was in the military. He didn't care much for me. All I heard growing up were war stories. All his buddies were military guys, so that's all they had to talk about. But fuck, I got tired of it. I mean, how many times are you going to look at pictures of dead Japs in Iwo Jima?

Dad never did any dad things with me. No school sports. No ball in the backyard. One time, we played catch in the yard, and he sprained his ankle. Who the fuck sprains their ankle just tossing a ball around? He just wasn't into being a father like that. He didn't care if I played baseball or did anything like that. (Don't think I didn't notice, though, that when my sister started cheerleading for the basketball team, he never missed a game.)

I'm the first and only boy, so I did boy things. We spent almost 10 years in Lebanon, Indiana—a town that now has about 15,000 people and is about 50 miles from Anderson. It was 1950s middle America in those parts--working-class families in homes on lots surrounding a small center of town. As kids, we just did normal stuff. Kite flying in the summer, sledding in the winter time, killing small animals out in the country, just normal things boys would do. We had a big family—grandparents, aunts, uncles. So every Thanksgiving, all the man-folk would go out hunting. Fun times. One time, I was walking through a field with one of my great uncles. I had never had a kill at that point.

"Gary, stop," he said. "Look over there. See that dark spot. That's a rabbit's eye. Shoot that."

Incredible vision, he had. That was my first kill.

Those days, we'd go back to the house, and the women would be cooking big feasts. They were great, family days. In the summertime, we'd go fishing all weekend long. My grandpa would get up at 4 in the morning, buy a whole bunch of minnows as bait, so we could get the first bite of the morning. Morning bite. Nothing like it. Even as I got older, we had a boat and I'd spend as much time on the water as I could. Shit, I probably spent more time on the water than I did on land. (As I got older, a lot of alcohol was involved. I didn't even know you could fish *without* alcohol.)

My first girlfriend—I was maybe 7 or 8—got killed by her dog. The dog leapt at her, and latched onto her jugular. Killed her, devastated me. It wasn't until recently that I realized that's probably the reason why I never really liked dogs that much, even now.

My grandpa, Grandpa Victor Hyatt (not the Nazi one), was my hero. He once told me he got kicked out of fourth grade for smoking cigarettes. He died from smoking, so it was probably true. Grandpa Hyatt wasn't a religious person. I never knew him to drink, but every Wednesday, he and his friends—we were told—always played poker. I assumed, of course, that they were playing poker, but I came to find out that he was actually at an AA meeting every week. Nobody told me that he used to drink but didn't drink anymore.

One day, when working in Grandpa Hyatt's shop, I found these little blue-covered, black-and-white books of porn in his toolbox. It was about eight pages with explicit cartoons—eight-page Bibles they're called. I took these things back into the bathroom and did what seventh-grade boys do when they see this stuff. Well, I stole one, and an exchange student from Iceland who was in my class wanted to buy it. I sold it to him for 50 cents. Come to think of it, that was my first contraband. Little did I know the life that would unfold after that.

So when the Iceland kid started passing it around to show other kids in the class, the teacher spotted it when some girl was looking at it while taking a science test. The teacher asked where it came from, and eventually I got ID'd as the hooligan who brought the naked pictures into school. Little fucker tracing it back to me.

I tried protesting since I sold it to the Iceland boy. "It ain't mine anymore!"

The school called my mom, and she picked me up. So she told me I had to 'fess up to my grandpa.

"Grandpa," I said. "I got kicked out of school because I stole one of your comic books and I sold it for 50 cents."

His response: "Sounds like a red-blooded American boy to me."

My first contraband, yes, but it was also my first entrepreneurial success.

Grandpa died in 1962 when I was a sophomore in high school, and it devastated me. I had just spent the weekend with him a couple days before he died, so it caught me totally off-guard, since it was my first death of a family member. And I lost my fishing buddy.

Around the time I was in middle school, we had moved back to Anderson from Lebanon, but my sister, who was two grades younger than I was, was going to a school where there were black people. My dad, who would swear up and down that he wasn't racist, didn't want his daughters going to school with any black kids, so we moved out to a 120-acre farm in a little village outside of town called Markleville (population under 1,000). In the summers, I'd work the farms. Hard farm work. We didn't make any money, just helped the family farms keep on running.

We were just mean little boys—like sic dogs on cats. That's what you're supposed to do, right? It's probably one of the reasons why I have cats now and am so nice to them—to try to make amends for the feline population I tormented as a kid.

Around Halloween time, my friends and I would go hide out in the corn field along the highways, clobbering vehicles with corn on the cob. Every night, a U.S. mail truck would drive through, and we'd lie in waiting for that fucking truck, just getting ready to hurl corn on the cob at it. God, he was so mad and tried to catch us every time.

One night, the mail truck driver hooked up with some law enforcement to try to catch us.

After we threw it, they stopped and started chasing us through the cornfields. We were on a dead fucking run trying to get out of the vision from their headlights. That cop knew we were out there. But we got away.

Later, we went to town and the cop was there. He walked up to me and started picking the burrs off my shirt.

"What have you boys been doing? he said. That fucker knew. "I'm gonna catch you one of these days."

They never did, thank God, because that's a federal offense—attacking a U.S. mail truck. Not that we knew. We just thought we're fucking throwing corn.

That was probably my first run-in with the law.

I was an average student. Nothing special. I never excelled at anything. Just survived. All the way through—grade school, middle school, high school—teachers were on my butt all the time about making better grades. They knew something about me that I didn't know about myself: *You should be in honor society, you should be an A student, you shouldn't be failing in math,* crap like that. I wasn't a good student, and I almost didn't graduate because I plagiarized an English lit term paper my senior year (it was easy to catch the fact I copied off my sister; in a school of 500 from grades 1 to 12, the teacher sure did think my paper sounded familiar).

At 16, I was given a choice for the first time in my life. I was never given the ability to make a choice about anything. But then, I was told I could decide whether I wanted to go to both church services on Sunday or just one. That was my first real choice in life. First one at 16 fucking years old. That's not the way to raise kids. If you don't teach a young person how to make good choices, look what happens. They turn into me!

I just wasn't motivated in school. The only thing that got me excited was President John F. Kennedy, Jr. His politics, his energy, his race to the moon. He was just an inspirational figure for all the young people in America. I created a rocket club in 1962, and I learned to create my own rocket fuel for the rockets we'd build in shop class. It was cool as hell. We'd set these things off in the big fields with these long fuses, light 'em up, and launch them. Had no idea where they landed. (If a kid did that today, they'd go to jail for terrorism.) We were all fucking devastated when JFK was killed.

I didn't really drink much, and I never really played hooky. I was much more interested in chasing girls, as all of us country boys were.

Hell, for as long as I can remember, I was a hound. As a little boy, I'd crawl around looking up girls' dresses, and things didn't change as I got older. We'd always be trying to look up skirts, chase girls, and get together. I went to church camp, and I had one goal in my mind: It had nothing to do with finding God. I wanted to fuck, even if I didn't know what it was. I remember my sister catching me trying to play doctor with a neighborhood girl out in our back garden when I was in something like fourth grade. And when I got old enough to buy a car, I bought one with a big back seat while my friends bought ones they could drag-race with. While they were racing, I was fucking.

I wanted pussy ever since I came out of one.

CHAPTER 2

DON'T KILL HIM! DON'T KILL HIM!

That's what teenage boys do, right?

Our whole world revolves around chasing girls, making out, and having sex. That's what I wanted, and I'd much rather skirt-chase than study hard.

In high school, I met Kathy, and she became my high school sweetheart. She was a hometown girl, and we went to school all through our time in Markleville. She was a shorty—5-foot-2—and blonde-haired. She was an honors student and played trumpet in the band.

We started to date in high school and yeah, we did all the things that kids in high school do. If you wanted to make out, you had to go park on a country road. We'd sit in her driveway after our dates, and after 10 minutes, the light would start flashing on her porch. We were watched closely.

In the one-stoplight town—which was an old, old, old farm village—the guys would hang out and compare notes about their conquests. That was life in Markleville, Indiana.

Her dad Ermel owned a big garage and had a tractor trailer that ran from Indiana to the south, mainly hauling meat to military bases there and bringing produce back. He eventually bought two trucks, then five. (He was probably up to a lot of shit that I didn't know about at the time. Who knows what he was hauling in those trucks?) Kathy did all the books for her dad. Ermel didn't like me very much. He told her to stay away from me—he didn't like the way I drove around town. I was a crazy kid after all.

My family was a bunch of teetotalers. Kathy's? They were drinkers. So I spent as much time with her family as I could because it was the only place I was allowed to drink. I hung out there a lot. We spent a lot of time on lakes, water skiing and having fun. We'd watch movies, play cards, just do family things that I never got to do with my family. They were a happy family, and I liked hanging there with them. This is the way people who didn't go to church lived, I thought. There was *life* in that family. My family just *existed*.

My family had the poor mentality, so we couldn't do anything— no, no, no, no, no. All the time.

I made it through high school okay, but not without some scars.

My last years at home, I slept on the couch because our home had caught fire, we got a new place that had three bedrooms—and my sisters got those, which was fine.

My dad didn't spend much time at home. He didn't like raising kids. Oh, he liked fucking and making kids. He loved his daughters, but me, not so much. Not at all.

He was on my ass my whole life. He thought he had to be a task master to be a good dad, and in his eyes, I never did anything to please that man. With anything. Severe fucking disciplinarian.

One time during winter, my car slipped on an icy road, and I hit a telephone pole turning into my driveway. It wasn't serious, but I dinged the car up. Dad came home, saw it, and started riding my ass. I was in the bathroom shaving, and I had had it. He was just ragging me and ragging me. So I turned around and slapped him in the head.

That man put me on the floor and beat the holy fuck out of me.

Punched me everywhere. Face, head, body. On the floor just wailing on me.

"Don't kill him! Don't kill him!" my mom yelled from the top of the staircase.

That was the only time I ever hit him, but it was the moment I never cared for my father ever again.

After I graduated, it was time to leave. Back then, when boys finished high school, they left. And I did. I graduated high school in 1964, and I moved out of the house and in with my grandma after signing up at Ball State University to keep from getting drafted. I went there that summer and fall, but I was not motivated to be a student. I was getting C's and D's. Hell, I was just there to keep from getting drafted. I got a job at the GM factory working the assembly line making alternators—5,000 alternators over an eight-hour shift. Brutal. You sat in the same fucking chair all that time with maybe a 20-minute lunch and two 10-minute breaks. Every 5 seconds, the line would move and I'd have to pick up a coil with three leads on it and put it on the studs on this other part and start the screws on it. We had to move fast, and it was hard work. It's no surprise that every fucking guy who worked on the line was a drinker.

When I started at Ball State, I worked an 11 p.m. to 7 a.m. shift and then get to a 7:30 a.m. class 20 miles away. I knew I couldn't keep up with that.

One of my relatives who worked there got me into the tool maker apprenticeship program, which would also keep me out of the draft. But I couldn't do both college and this program.

I asked the draft review board what my options were, and they said that I could do the apprentice program and if I could reach 1,000 required hours, I would still get my four-year deferment. "And if you're close when you get your draft notice," they told me, "we'll take that into consideration."

When I got my draft notice, I had 880 of the 1,000 hours completed, so figured I was in good shape, considering what they had told me about being close. I needed three more weeks to get the four-year deferment. So I took it to the board.

They said, "Too bad, you're going."

On February 6, 1966, I was drafted.

At the recruitment and induction center in Indianapolis, some soldier made an announcement.

"We need seven volunteers to go to San Diego TONIGHT."

My arm couldn't shoot up fast enough. San Diego? Sun, beach? Hell yes. Get me out of Cold as Fuck, Indiana, and this god-awful weather. Well, this assignment was for the Marines and we'd be sent straight to Vietnam. They gave us some tests, and an hour later, they came out and said right to my face: "You're too smart for your size to be a Marine. You can't go to San Diego."

What the fuck. It's the first time in my life anyone has ever called me smart. I'm too smart to be a Marine? I figured it out quick: The Marines were just looking for big, dumb motherfuckers who'd be just fine taking orders.

So I went to basic training in Fort Knox, Kentucky. That's where they did all kinds of tests, trying to figure out where you'd fit best in the military, personality profiling, shit like that. It was rigorous but good. This country does a good job preparing soldiers to be ready to fight.

One day, the officers called about 20 of us out of formation. I had an open mind, but I knew I didn't want to go to Vietnam.

"You guys are qualified to get into missile electronics. You can go to school for a year."

"Fuck, that sounds pretty cool," I thought. "Let's go look at it." Here I'm thinking that if I spend a year in school, that's a year I *don't* have to spend in Vietnam. But there was a catch. If you did the school, you'd have to change your status from a draftee (a two-year stint) to regular Army (a mandatory three years). I took it and signed on for an extra year.

In the recruiter's office, they showed me a thick-ass catalog of all of their different missiles. Tons of them. When he flipped through, I asked him the same question over and over, "Is that in Vietnam or will it ever go?" And if he said yes, I told him to turn the page. Not that one, no thanks.

Halfway through the book, we got to a certain missile. He said, "Nope, it's not in Vietnam and it never will go."

"That's the school I want," I said.

And that's what I got. It was an 18-week course in Huntsville, Alabama, in our space center. A very exciting time to be there, for sure. Every third cycle, we'd get an extra 18 weeks of training. Top graduates got more training, and I was one of them. It was really intense stuff. You had to know every part and piece—all of it (and re-member, this is before digital systems, so it was all analog). I fucking got competitive as fuck, trying to beat out some cocky weasel who thought he was the smartest motherfucker there. Well, I dusted him, and I got special privileges to take my Friday test and finish early, so I could have a three-day pass off base.

When I was in Huntsville, I didn't like living in the barracks. And the only way to get out of the barracks was to be married. So I went home on a weekend pass, bought an engagement ring for Kathy, and proposed. She was still living at home.

She said yes.

CHAPTER 3

A MARRIAGE OF CONVENIENCE

Kathy was thrilled. I was not.

For me, the proposal was just to get out of barracks. She was a useful tool in my development, but fuck, that's not the reason to get married—and I knew that our marriage was doomed for failure from the very beginning. After I proposed, I came back to Alabama, and one night I was out drinking with the guys. I met a girl there I was head over heels for. Like crazy. Like she gave me a spark I had never felt.

Later, I called my mother.

"Mom, I'm calling this wedding off. I don't love Kathy. It would be wrong to marry her. I thought I did."

Mom and Dad wouldn't let me. They drove to Huntsville, Alabama, physically put me in the car and drove me back to Indiana.

I didn't want to be there, but I couldn't fight back or else my father would beat me. He didn't want to be shamed, so there was nothing I could do to get out of it.

And I got married—at 18 years old—in August 1966.

I stood there in church, and my pant leg was visibly moving my legs were shaking so bad.

I knew I was making the first big mistake in my life. That's how scared I was. And that's how sure I was that I fucked this up. I knew this was wrong. All because I didn't want to live in the fucking barracks.

I put on a show and made the best of it. I had told my friends that my dad wouldn't let me get out of it.

"That's not a reason to get married," they said.

"I know," I said, "but I don't have a fucking choice."

That's a fucked-up thing if you think about it, for your parents to force you to get married so *they* wouldn't be embarrassed.

The fact of the matter was that my dad was not going to look bad in a small town by his son leaving someone at the altar. It was him making me be a responsible human being and keep my word.

Which is sort of funny now, because after I got drafted, my own parents split up. Mom got a job working at RCA—first time she ever had a job because she was never allowed to work. She ended up falling in love with a black man who worked at RCA. Boy, would that send some of my racist relatives through a loop. Mom left Indiana and went to California; they couldn't live as a mixed couple in Indiana. They had a rocky relationship. In California, my mom got a job at a securities agency. She had tons of unregistered securities at her desk, so she knew nobody would know if she took one or two, so she started stealing. James was greedy and wanted her to do more and more. She got busted. They both got busted. They were both sentenced to a year for the crimes in their 40s. They ended up staying together for 27 years before she died, and he died shortly after that. Cancer of the dick, if you can believe that. Later, my sisters found some of their old letters and learned that James had fathered four children with different women.

My dad remarried to a woman named Betty, who had a large family. And she wanted us all to be a big, happy family. Like, she wanted her kids to call me their brother. Fuck, I don't fucking know you. I'm not buying into that shit. She was just a mean, nasty bitch. Well, Betty died, and then my dad married Alma, the hairdresser.

Alma was a crazy lady who couldn't be satisfied sexually. That's all she wanted to do. Have sex. Dad didn't have sex the last five years with Betty, so he sort of felt like he was at a loss. Yeah, he had four children, but he was so religiously controlled that he didn't know a damn thing about satisfying such a sexually charged woman as Alma. In fact, when dad was newly married, he asked me this: "I'm having trouble performing. Any suggestions?"

I was so sickened by it all. Later in their life, she wouldn't get off his lap—like an 80-year-old woman and kept saying to my dad, "You can't satisfy me, you can't satisfy me!" I wanted to smack her. When my dad died at 82, I cleaned out his house and I found in his drawer a copy of the kama sutra book—1,001 ways to have sex or some shit like that. Jesus, I thought. And I took it out to Alma and said, "What the hell is this?"

"We tried all those!" she said to me.

But I'm getting ahead of myself. The point is that my dad was telling me all the shit I should do, and here his relationships have been fucked up since the day he told my mom that she would learn to love him.

Before Kathy and I got married, I had rented a house, and for two months before Kathy moved in, a buddy of mine who also joined the military lived with me. He was a poker player. And he told me that we could make some money by hosting poker games. I would supply the beer and snacks as the host—and I'd get 10 percent of the pot in return.

During that time, I fell in love with another woman from Huntsville who I met at a bar, after I had bought an engagement ring for Kathy. I had been with this bartender for four or five months. But after I got married, this woman would come by the house, honk her horn, and make me come out and talk to her. She was devastated that I was married, and I was devastated—but there was nothing I could do. Fuck if I can remember her name, but I remember her large breasts and long legs and that she had one long hair on her nipple. I had never seen that before.

After my training, I was assigned to go to Germany.

I didn't want to go there—mainly because I knew that if I was assigned Germany, I had to take Kathy. If I was assigned Korea, I wouldn't be allowed to take my wife, so I wanted to go to Korea.

Denied.

I spent two years in Germany on the border of Czechoslovakia. My job: Make all the missiles work. Make every component of our missile work. We were highly skilled technicians who had to keep the missiles flying, so we worked every day.

At first, because of a misassignment, I was sent to an artillery unit in Frankfurt. They had no missiles, just some dirty bombs, which weren't very accurate weapons. One of the first things I had to do was go out in the woods as part of an inspection with an M-80 machine gun. I had to go out in the middle of the night and "run point" on the border. There, we had to learn how to dig foxholes and shit. I dug a hole deep enough for my sleeping bag to fit.

Then I took a wire and made three perimeters around my area with Coke cans on them. I put rocks in them, so if anyone came by there in the middle of the night, I'd hear 'em coming when they rattled the cans. This is the first time I felt like I was really playing soldier.

In the middle of the night, when I was sleeping, I heard the cans rattle and someone cussing like hell. Then it happened again. So I had to check it out.

It was the fucking general doing an inspection.

I ended up getting a three-day pass for noticing him sneaking up on us—all for being an exceptional soldier. Ha, fuck me, I just wanted to get some sleep.

A couple months later, I got assigned to the place I was supposed to be—in Scwhabisch Hall, near Stuttgart. Beautiful part of Germany.

I had made friends with Walter, the taxi driver who picked me up at the train station. Walter had been a POW in WWII and spoke fluent French and English, and we became best of friends while I was there. We even spent holidays together. He took me all around town to all the guests houses around town. Every one of them—I mean every single one of them—had a drink named after Walter. Three shots of cognac, one shot of Coke. That was his drink. And he drank it all… day… long. It's one of the ways I assimilated into the German culture. He helped me find cars, apartments, everything. It was so cheap to live there. I bought furniture, and in 1967, I bought a 1957 Mercedes for $300. I also traded a lot, since I could get stuff on the military base that Germans couldn't get, like refrigerators, ice cream, fucking American whiskey.

Walter introduced me to some of his friends—a prison guard and his wife, who was a seamstress. They had young kids and built an apartment on the top floor of their house. I rented it in a quaint village near the base. Loved that place. They had a bathtub in the kitchen—they'd put a lid on it so it could be a bench during the day. We didn't have a refrigerator, so we'd sit our milk and butter out on the window sill during the winter.

At the base, I got permission to bring Kathy over. We had been married for a year by that time.

During my stay in Germany, we made decent money, as Kathy was working at the PX. We lived off the base, traveled around Europe, and had a good time. I had a good rank—staff sergeant E5— and worked in a sports bar in the evenings. And I had a 10-year-old Mercedes with velvet seats that I bought for $300. Wrecked that sucker on ice.

At the sports bar, we just drank and drank and drank. How could you not with 10-cent beers? Fuck.

Epic drinking went on in that place.

And just the whole culture was all about drinking—cases delivered to your home, cheap beers in the bar. Everybody drank alcohol. They even served kids some wine in their juices. It's just what they did.

One time early on in Germany, a sergeant turned to us all and said, "Real soldiers eat glass." And he picked up a glass and took a bite out of it.

We all started doing it. Hell, the thin pilsner glasses weren't bad. As long as you didn't cut your tongue on the way in, you were ok. My buddy and I were known in the bar—me for eating glasses, him for arm wrestling.

In Germany, Kathy and I tried to make the best of it. We traveled all over Germany, we had cash, we ate out all the time, we made the most of it. I didn't chase other women. Before Kathy got there, I had been with a couple German girls, but I stopped. Walter introduced me to one of the largest tile installers in the country (he had a full-size bar and entertainment area in his house—pool tables and everything). I helped him by getting him American whiskey, coffee, and stuff like that. He had a daughter. And I'll leave it at that.

But Kathy and I did keep trying to make it work, and I didn't get with other women when she was there.

One time, we went to London when the mini-skirt craze started. I left there with black-and-blue marks on my arm from Kathy elbowing me for looking at girls' asses hanging out like I had never seen before (the craze hadn't hit the U.S. yet).

Kathy and I did have our intimacy issues, and looking back, I think they stemmed from the fact that she and her sisters had been sexually molested by a relative and I was sworn to secrecy on it. I couldn't live with that secret; the family was protecting a family molester. But just her talking about it helped us for a time. Kathy felt liberated and became much more sexually uninhibited after she told me about it.

One night, after a big beer festival, the two of us were drunk. We wanted to have sex, but Kathy told me it probably wasn't a good time in her cycle pregnancy-wise. I said, aw hell, we haven't gotten pregnant yet, so what the fuck, let's fuck. (And, of course, Kathy got pregnant. My son was made in Germany but born in the United States after we returned.)

When we lived in Germany, we just drank a ton. Even when you could be on call at any minute to come fix something, you could've been drunk as shit. My heavy drinking had really started in basic training—away from home for the first time and all.

Even back then, one of my sergeants said to me, "You got to quit drinking. You're going to get in trouble."

That's also about the time that I did my first dealing when a man approached me and asked me this: "If you give me $400 today and I give you back $700 in a few days, would you do it?" And I asked him how the hell he would do that. He told me he needed a front to buy some hash that he'd sell and we'd both make profits from it. I had the money, so I said, sure, why not? I wasn't interested in smoking it, but I was interested in making more money. Every month on pay day, I'd give this guy his front and then he'd flip it for more.

I couldn't imagine wanting to smoke that stuff. Why would anybody want to smoke marijuana when they could have Jim Beam? That was my thinking because it was all about the booze. That's how I felt for years and years. Never did partake over there.

But I learned immediately: There is money to be made in this business.

If I had decided to reenlist in the Army and stay for another six years to go to warrant officer school and be stationed in Vicenza, Italy, my bonus would have been $12,000. That certainly would have been enough to buy the $6,000 Porsche 911T I had my eye on when I was there and visited the Porsche factory in Stuttgart. Hell, I could have bought two Porsches.

Ultimately, though, I decided I couldn't do it. I couldn't do the military thing anymore. I never questioned the chain of command, and I never took a wrong step. But I had a problem with the military mindset—and the authoritarian way of living. We all put our pants on the same way, we all followed orders, we all have to bow down to some fucking idiot because they've got some stars on their uniforms? Fuck. I'm not going to have some idiot whose ranked higher than me (and dumber than me) telling me to paint shit. Because that's what we did when there was nothing else to do—paint shit. If it doesn't move, paint it. That style of living just wasn't me. I didn't want to make the military my career, though I did seriously consider it.

So I got my discharge, got out in December 1968, and started back at Ball State in January 1969. I went back there because I had three years of the GI Bill, so college was paid for. I decided I wanted to be a lawyer and a politician, which is I why I decided to study political science, American history, and sociology. I also wanted to get my teacher's certificate, so I could teach my way through law school. That was my plan. I still had my job at GM waiting for me, and I did that while going to school full-time, and I helped my father-in-law in his trucking business and helping distribute watermelons from fields he bought in Florida and truck them back to Indiana.

Just before I got discharged from the Army, Brown University in Birmingham, Alabama, offered me a full-ride electrical engineering scholarship—a co-op where you'd go to school for six months and work for six months. I probably would have gone there if it wasn't in Alabama. I turned it down because I decided I wanted to be a lawyer and a politician. It was one of those decisions where you look back and say, fuck, maybe I shouldn't have turned it down. I thought being a lawyer or politician would have been an honorable profession. Looking back, I can't believe I thought *that*.

I went to Ball State through 1971 and sold life insurance, because one of my professors recruited me into the business. Kathy worked as a secretary. The insurance business was proving to be promising. I was selling policies and for every single one that I sold, I'd get $1,000 a year off of it. This could have been career I was building—and probably the best chance I had of doing well considering where I was from and the lack of opportunities in small-town, Indiana.

All this time, I was drinking heavily. Beer, liquor, all of it.

The reality was that I was a high-functioning alcoholic—raising a family, working two jobs, going to school, and just drinking and drinking. Beer, hard alcohol, didn't matter. I generally drank after my afternoon classes and before my night class. That gave me several hours to drink and go to class drunk as shit. I was an obstinate drunk. I'll argue about anything. In one political science class, the professor was a former diplomat, and I argued with him so badly that I couldn't even go back to class because I embarrassed myself so badly.

One of my military buddies was going to school and partied in Chicago and introduced me to street speed. I really liked amphetamines because that meant you could drink forever. Anything that could help me drink more was great. Study, stay up, drink. I was all in it.

Kathy was not.

One night after finals, I was headed home—20-some miles from campus. We had been eating speed for three days studying for finals. I stopped at a bar near home and called a friend and told him I was feeling really, really fucked up. He came over to help, but I had already left.

I left that bar, headed home, slid on black ice around a curve and slammed the right front of the car into an abutment of a railroad tunnel. I didn't even remember being on the road—I was near dead, crunched up against the steering wheel. The speedometer had stopped on 53 mph—head-on to a cement wall on black ice. One of my classmates had a boyfriend who was on the rescue, and he told her that I had died at the scene. (Imagine her face when I walked back in class a few weeks later.)

I was in a coma for three days. When I woke up, my mom and sister were there (my mom was living in California at the time). I needed my jaw sewn up, and my knee was all banged up. I fucked up my arm and was in a cast for four months, with surgeries and plates and shit, so I had to learn to do everything left-handed. It didn't slow me down then, and I still feel that injury in my arm today.

Even that didn't make me quit drinking. Nothing did.

At Ball State, I smoked my first pot. I was at a party with some hippies and they had some. It was fun, but I was a little scared of the conversation they were having. They were all talking about the alphabet of drugs—LSD, PCP, everything. I thought they were crazy, but I did get a bag of pot from them to take with me. I enjoyed the getting stoned part and wanted to do some more.

Nobody wanted to smoke it with me. I ended up throwing that bag away.

As you might imagine, my relationship with Kathy was not in good standing. I was in college and having a great time. I was good-looking and loved women.

In fact, I was fucking everything that moved. If it wiggled, I went after it. All through my life, I slept around. It must have been dozens of women during this time in my life.

One time, shortly after we had gotten back from Germany, I was in school, and we were hanging out with a couple that we knew from Germany. They were making their way through Indiana, so they stopped by. Something clicked between his wife and me. The electricity was off the charts. We wanted to fuck so bad.

We didn't right then (we were in my house after all), but we both knew that's what we wanted. And all of my spark, my energy, and my lust was directed toward that woman—not my wife.

When the couple left, I just decided: I couldn't stay married anymore.

I didn't love Kathy, so I packed my car, and I decided I was going to go meet this other woman in Oregon, where she was headed. (We had spent time with her and her husband in Germany and stayed friends with them.)

In the garage with the car running and ready to go, Kathy came out and got on her knees. She begged me. "Please, don't leave. You can do anything you want. Just don't leave."

Fuck. So I stayed.

Why did I stay? I don't know. I guess when your wife says that you can do whatever you want and sleep with whoever you want, you think that's a pretty decent offer.

Here I am, in college, just out of the Army, I've got a nice car, and there were all these sorority girls around. Pussy everywhere. We went all the damn time to a bar called Mr. B's Lounge. I joined an independent fraternity, and we didn't do a damn thing except drink. One night, I even stole the Ball State marching band banner out of the gym. I held onto that thing for a long, long time. I wonder whatever happened to it. Maybe I should check eBay or something.

You know how bad it got? One time, I even fucked a woman who worked right next to Kathy in her office. I went to college with that woman's husband, hung out with him, and played golf with him. But he worked the night shift. I didn't.

And that woman was a horny little thing. She'd scratch my back up during sex, and Kathy would see it. I'd tell her exactly who did it.

It was cold and callous—and just damn cruel when you think about it. But fuck, she's the one who wanted to stay married even when I didn't. I told her as much, and she told me to screw whoever I wanted. I did.

I was trying to make Kathy hate me and force her hand to throw me out. So I fucked the woman she worked with. But she really *couldn't* say a thing. When I look on it now, I think the real reason why I couldn't stay with Kathy was that I couldn't deal with the fact that Kathy's family had protected a child molester all this time. It just ate at me that the whole family had let that go on without doing a thing, when all I wanted to do was go over there and kill him. So I took it out by sleeping around and trying to get Kathy to kick me out. And she never did.

Finally, I couldn't live with myself anymore. I had to go.

In May 1971, I met my dad at the track at the Indianapolis Speedway to watch the practice rounds for the Indy 500. I told him I had had enough.

"Dad, if I don't leave Indiana, somebody's gonna shoot me," I told him.

"Why?"

"I'm fucking a whole bunch of married women and their husbands don't like it," I said.

"Why you doing that?" he darted back.

"Because you made me marry a woman I didn't love," I said. "and I gotta get out of here."

He tried to talk me out of leaving. But he couldn't do it, and I couldn't take it.

And that's when I got in my car, took my stuff—and my life—down to Florida for the adventure of a lifetime.

CHAPTER 4

QUACK QUACK BEACH

The year before I left Kathy, I had traveled to Florida, where we stayed in a pop-up camper for two weeks. During that time, I went out on a party boat, and I had caught the biggest fish and the most fish I ever had. And I just loved it. I couldn't spend any more time in that nasty-winter weather in Indiana, and I knew I had to get back down there. Because my drinking and skirt-chasing was so bad, I had to leave. Here I had been doing all those things, trying to get Kathy to throw me out, but she never did. When we did split up, Kathy moved in with her aunt.

And I left.

I had an insurance job waiting for me in Florida. One of my professors at Ball State University had arranged it for me, so at least I had something in the works. A new start, I thought. Back in Indiana, I had started in that line of work and was making good money, so I figured that could give me a good base.

The minute I got out of Indiana and into Ohio, I bought a case of Busch tall boys and put them on ice as I started down the interstate coming down to Florida. I got pretty drunk, driving 90 or 100 mph. In Georgia, I even picked up a hitchhiker, but he asked me to let him out because he was so spooked by my drunk driving. Man, I was drunk as shit. I stopped with a family relative in Valdosta, Georgia, some 800 miles away from where I started, and I woke up with the nastiest hangover.

When I crossed into Florida, I got out the map and asked myself one question: what coast is closest?

I wanted to be in Florida, but I didn't know where I should make my landing point.

The closest was the west coast on the Gulf of Mexico, so I scooted over to Route 19 and just drove south.

I landed in St. Pete Beach in May 1971 and never left.

St. Pete Beach is a touristy, coastal town that occupies Long Key—a barrier island that borders the Gulf of Mexico. It's not too far from Clearwater and Tampa. As recently as 2021, St. Pete Beach—home of the historical hotel called The Don CeSar—was named the top beach in the U.S. and a top 5 beach in the world.

The day after I got there, I drove to Lakeland—about 60 miles away—to get my application for my state insurance license. When I got back to the beach, I met a woman staying in the same hotel as I was—crazy lady working as a gossip reporter. We had hung out at the bar the night before, and when I got back to the motel, she said, "Oh Gary, I got someone I want you to meet. He's got a job waiting for you."

The guy was running concessions on the beach, and yeah, he was looking for help. Didn't pay much, like 10 bucks a day, but he was also offering room and board. Fuck, I thought. Live on the beach, hang on the beach, get my expenses paid for? What the fuck, let's do this. I had it made.

So I started there five days after I arrived in Florida and never ever followed up on the insurance job. Life was cheap back in 1971. Hardly anybody lived there. The population was about 8,000 in the town of St. Pete Beach.

I worked there about six months. As part of the job, we'd rent out 14-foot Hobie cat sailboats for people on the beach. It took me all of about 10 minutes to learn how to sail, but that was my first sailing experience (who knew I'd be really sailing with tons of pot on a boat some years later). I learned the nuances of sailing boats with two hulls, and I learned how to catch a breeze and start flying a hull, as well as how to right yourself if you tip over. It was a lot of fun.

I adopted the beach life—running on the beach, living in the sun, having fun, feeling happy.

For the first time, I felt freedom. A born-again beach bum.

I could do what I wanted when I wanted, and that was something I constantly longed for, when you consider that during my whole life to that point, I was living in one constant state of accountability. My father. The military. My wife. Even though Kathy let me do what I wanted at the end of our marriage, I still was married and had the responsibility hanging over my head. So this was true freedom.

It was the first time I could stop and see what the world had to offer. My alcohol, of course, was out of control, as it had been as soon as I started drinking. Add in the fact that I was now by myself living the good life in a beach town? Fuck. Recipe for a constant state of drunkenness.

My landlord hated it. She'd yelled at me, calling me a drunk. I mostly drank beer and wine because it was cheap. No need to have the hard stuff when you could get the buzz you needed with beer and wine. So I drank it, lots of it. Fuck. Busch beer was $1.99 a case. Can you imagine—24 beers for two bucks? We'd drink at least a case a day.

I made good friends back then. We lived and played and partied. We ate well, too, because some of the guys would steal steaks from the market, and we'd cook those up. Cheap living, for sure. We played pool, hung out on the beach, fought with cops even (one time, my buddies spent a couple years in prison for a fight with cops in a bar that started because the cops didn't like cussing).

On the beach, I started meeting girls, hung out with them, and then met a guy who sold me my first weed. This was my first real experience with it. I had bought it that one time at Ball State, but nobody would smoke it with me, so I threw it away.

I bought a couple bags—turned out to be Missouri River funk weed, headache weed. Damn. But I didn't know any better at the time.

After I settled into St. Pete Beach, just about all of the people I knew worked in the pot business. We were hippies hanging out on the beach, drinking Bud and Busch, smoking weed, fishing, riding boats. Most of us held some kind of service job in a bar or something like that so we had some income to file taxes, but most of our money came from selling weed.

We spent almost every day in a spot we called Quack Quack Beach. We named it that because we just hung out there all day quack quack quack quack. We hung a keg from a tree. Girls rolled the joints. Guys fucked around on boats and dirt bikes and water skis. We were shooting the shit quack quack quack. Doing dope quack

quack quack. Hanging and jiving and shucking quack quack quack. We brought our dogs, and the sheriff's office would drive by and ask if everything was cool. It was. We didn't usually drink before noon. We were responsible like that. We were just hanging out living a free, fuck-the-feds life, selling pot, and making good money.

Ever since I started smoking pot and dealing it, I knew I wanted more from this life. A bigger role. An adventure. I wanted to be more than a hippie hanging out. I wanted to be *in* the business.

I wanted to smuggle.

It was a romantic notion, really. What's better than giving people the weed they wanted and having a hand in bringing all this good shit across the border to a country that wanted to arrest good people just wanting to live a happy, free, high life? Fuck the feds, and fuck everyone who had started this war on drugs.

It took me some time to figure out that the people I noticed on St. Pete Beach who were living large early in the 1970s were the ones who were smuggling. It was all brand new to me, but I did learn that these guys were the first ones bringing Caribbean weed to the U.S., and I quickly realized that I wanted to do that too.

I had been in St. Pete Beach for six months when I sent Kathy plane tickets to bring my son, Jason, and spend a long weekend there.

"If you want us to be together as a family, it's going to have to be here," I told Kathy. "I can't do it in Indiana. I'm never going back there."

That weekend, I saw a job opening at Honeywell Electronics. But right after she left, there was a job opening at a bar. I took that one and didn't take Honeywell. When I told Kathy that I took a job in a bar, I stopped hearing from her. And I wondered why, so I called and asked her.

"You didn't get your mail yet?" she said.

"No," I said.

"The papers are in the mail. I decided to divorce you."

"Fine," I said. "I'll just come to Indiana and get my son and bring him down to Florida. I'm not living in Indiana, and you don't have to raise my son."

Well that scared her. I think I may have even joked that I was going to bring him down to Barbados and teach him how to surf. Well, that really got her going. She had already asked me for child support, which is when I told her I'd get my son. But she remarried real quick—like within six months.

A notice appeared in the local paper in Indiana saying that I needed to appear in court to show why my son shouldn't be adopted or have his name changed. Well, I didn't see that fucking paper because I was in Florida. I didn't even find out about it until six months after it happened. I was in California in 1972 visiting my mother—first time in six years I had seen her. Because I missed that, I couldn't see my son until he was 18 years old (he was 9 at the time). At that point, I knew that if I ever went back to Indiana, I'd probably do something I'd regret for a long, long time. You don't do that to a person—take their kids away like that. I mean, I was an asshole, so I'm sure she felt like I deserved it.

Over the years, Kathy and I were civil with each other, and she would occasionally come to Florida. I had gotten my son into fishing so I could teach him some skills since he was always in trouble. Kathy and I got along ok. He came to live with me in 1987 when he was 18. Jason was a severe addict. Alcohol, cocaine, all of it. He and his girlfriend, who we called Dirtbag Debbie, were drunk and fucked up all the time. He always worked his mother and stepdad for money.

He worked them against each other to get money because he was spending his money on drugs—more than he had. Jason had Kathy convinced that he had quit all the bad stuff. When he died at age 37, I got the call, and when I told Kathy about his cause of death, she said didn't believe that he was still doing drugs—all because he had lied so much and so well. She was so upset that she didn't even want to come to the funeral. All his friends were fishermen. Fishing shut down in February, so I scheduled the memorial service at a church in Madeira Beach, which was nearby, and Kathy showed up. I didn't talk to her for a long, long time after that. But I do sometimes call her on Jason's birthday—and I think about her on that day every year.

CHAPTER 5

A SHOCKING DISCOVERY

All this time working in bars and living on the beach when I was starting out in the weed business, I wasn't just making friends. I was making weed contacts.

Nothing big. I'd buy a little, then start splitting it up and selling it.

It wasn't conscious decision or part of some master plan. You have some, people like it, they want some.

And that's one of the major universal truths I've learned in this life: You don't sell weed; weed sells itself.

When people know you sell, they flock to you.

Still true today.

The harsh reality of life is that the majority of Americans want to smoke weed. Even Christians.

We were all strangers living in the same period of time in a fucked-up world. The Vietnam War had a lot of us really fucked up. Then there were the Kent State shootings. That's when four students were killed and nine other unarmed students were killed by the National Guard during a peaceful rally of students protesting the U.S. involvement in the Vietnam War. It was political upheaval like we had never seen.

Smoking pot was one of the things that fucking helped.

Fuck the government. Fuck the police. Free love. Freedom to do drugs.

That's what people wanted. Make love, not war. (Plus, it's damn nice to make love when you're stoned.)

Weed was an expression of our freedom. Fuck you. We're not going to follow the rules. You're opposed to it? We're for it. You're for it? We're opposed to it.

The draft and Vietnam really did it—that horror show of a war we couldn't win really stoked that whole mentality. The people who came back from Vietnam, man, it was so fucked up. So scary. You could see the trauma of killing innocent people (and seeing their fellow American killed); it was all so fucking heartbreaking and earth-shattering. Back then, nobody fucking talked about PTSD. But we saw it. And we felt it.

In that era, people didn't know how to get weed all that well, and that's where we came in. You introduce yourself, they find out what you have ("what, whoa, you have some of *that*?"), and weed sells its-fucking-self. Always been that way, always will be.

All through that first year and a half in St. Pete Beach, I was partying, selling pot, working the bars. Nothing major was on my mind, though I did want that good life that came from more than just dealing in small amounts. I sure as shit didn't foresee myself sailing a boat to Colombia to pick up more than five tons of pot and smuggle it back to the U.S.

I started by buying little bits of pot. Here's how it works: You know a person selling and you buy an ounce, you break that into four quarters. You sell three quarters, which covers the price of the ounce, then you get to smoke the one quarter for free. That's how most pot transactions are done—still today.

I built my business really slow, working in the bar scene and meeting more people, like Stetson University law students and guys from the Coast Guard. In the bar scene, you get connected to a lot of people, so I met a guy who hooked me up with a painting job. That's the kind of job you need to have some legal income to live and pay your bills and cover up the fact that you're making the real money by selling drugs. The survival-type jobs.

One day, I was working on the roof of a two-story apartment building with a real rough stucco finish. I was holding a 12-foot aluminum extension handle and trying to dig into the crannies of the stucco. My boss was pointing to me where to go because I couldn't see.

He directed me right into a 7,200-volt power line.

Fuck. I don't remember that charge, but that kicked me into a 440-volt line, all while I was holding the aluminum handle.

Now on the edge of the roof with my knees bracing me against a lip, I started to go over, but somehow I was able to stop myself and ground myself. All the electricity fucking traveled through me, like my veins and arteries and bones are on massive subway system and the electricity is every train in the fleet going full throttle on every track.

I could feel my heart exploding. Some of my skin burned off, and my Seiko watch flamed a hole in my wrist.

The foreman raced up to me, "Are you alright?"

"No," I said. "My arms are completely paralyzed."

I told him to take my watch off immediately because I know that if I waited until I had feeling back, it would burn and hurt like a motherfucker when they tried to take it off.

It took forty-fucking-five minutes to get a rescue truck to me, and the two guys in the ambulance didn't have any ice when they started to take me to the hospital.

"Look," I said, "there's a cigarette pack in my shirt pocket. There's two big, ol' fat joints in there. Take one out and light it for me."

I smoked it the whole way–those two EMTs holding it for me— because I knew the pain was going to be horrible when the feeling came back.

I ended up in ICU for seven days and did recover. But here's where that shock really changed my life: Because that 7,200-volt power line was too close to the building, Florida Power & Light was liable for my injuries. They handed me a settlement check for something like 10 grand. It should have been much more, like hundreds of thousands, because I got fucked bad.

This was my entry into dealing in bigger-time circles. I took two thousand bucks and invested in five pounds of weed that I could sell. And that was my first step toward becoming a marijuana merchant. When I bought that first five pounds, I knew where I wanted it to lead—not just selling.

I wanted to smuggle.

CHAPTER 6

THE LADY WITH LONG, LONG LEGS

One day, a long-legged blonde woman walked into Red's Taproom, where I was tending bar, and I was like holy shit. Like *holy shit*. She was something.

Connie.

She was looking for an old boyfriend. She had photos of him and said he was riding a motorcycle. "Anybody seen him?" she asked. Nobody knew the guy.

She left the bar, and I knew that I had to find her before she found her old boyfriend.

When Connie left, I took notice. She said she was staying at a motel along the beach, so I saw what kind of car she was driving. A 1971 Buick. After work, I drove up and down that beach looking for that car.

When I found it, I knocked on the door and immediately started wooing Connie.

Connie was from Maryland, outside of D.C. Her father worked for the State Department, and her mom was a nice lady from West Virginia. Connie had done secretarial work in D.C., and we hit it off right from the start.

We hooked up, and she loved everything I was doing, including the dealing. Connie and I stayed together—six years, in fact. And we used all of our contacts to sell weed up and down the coast. (We ended up marrying after I got arrested in New York, mostly to look good for the judge and the legal system.)

After I won her over, she moved in with me, and we started being together all the time. Working, partying, socializing, doing acid, drinking wine, being hippies.

Connie's only problem? Sometimes, she'd get violent.

She liked eating barbiturates and drinking alcohol, and she got so fucking mean when she did. She tried to run me over sometimes. She didn't take much shit from me.

We just were going with the flow, but after my accident when I got shocked, I started thinking about a bigger life—the life I saw the dealers having on the beach. The nice cars, the nice women, the partying, the dream.

I got my garage apartment on the beach, owned by a crazy old wino lady who lived in front. I worked at one bar where all the Coast Guard hung out and then one where all the hippies hung out. Tending bar, making sandwiches, living the beach life.

All this time as I was starting out, I'd be getting my weed from Jamaica and Colombia. There was so much of it. Most times, I'd have

500 to 1,000 pounds of it at a time. But we weren't making that much money because it seemed like everybody had some and was selling it.

Selling wasn't that much work. Connie usually had a job, but my days were party days. We were into LSD. Hell, we'd eat acid and drink cheap-ass wine all day.

At one point, I was living in a house in Gulfport, Florida, that had one time been the temporary home of Yogi Berra, Mickey Mantle, Joe DiMaggio, and Whitey Ford, because the Yankees had spring training there. The little old lady who lived next door told me stories about them. These were my fucking heroes growing up, and here I am, living in their spring training home. Cool as shit. I was eating a lot of orange-sunshine LSD so the world always looked orange to me.

I kept 500 pounds of weed in a room back there in big burlaps sacks.

Back then, I was getting Jamaican weed for $65 a pound (hell, today you pay $50 a quarter ounce). I was selling pounds for maybe $75 to $100 depending on the quality, so I wasn't making a lot. All of it was seeded—lots of seeds in it. People have since learned that you can kill the boys so the female plants produce resin, instead of seeds. (And that's what all weed is today, since nobody likes seed in their weed, unless you find one and try to grow it yourself, since one seed could grow a pound of pot.) We were always looking for new markets. And somebody was always getting busted for pot.

Red's Taproom, back then, was called the Den of Iniquity of Pinellas County for all the bad stuff we'd do. The place was a horseshoe-shaped bar—typical dive bar with pool tables, games, that kind of stuff.

It was just a big party scene, and for a lot of the time, there really wasn't much the cops could do. Smoking and sex was happening on the public beaches, and sometimes, cops would come up and take the weed from them (but at the time, it was local cops—no real DEA or major enforcement going on there). From my perspective, it was just a bunch of unified, beach-life, free spirits running around, not worrying about the laws, not being constrained, just living free. You know, the fuck-the-world youth—and the spirit that comes from that type of thinking.

One night when I was first starting out, cops came to my house. We were sitting out drinking and smoking. This was right after my first big investment of five pounds.

"Ok, where's all the drugs? We need the drugs."

They left because they didn't have a warrant and just waited outside my house. I thought they were waiting to get a warrant, and I was freaking out because it was my first big investment. I had a Wise potato chip can near my toilet filled with a pound of weed, so I was ready to dump it and the four pounds that were in the trunk of my car. When I got ready to trash it, I looked out the window and the cops had left. Damn.

But it was enough to scare me, so I took the weed and hid it under the porch of the bar where I worked.

I walked back whistling, happy, so I called the cops when I got back home.

"Hey, we're waiting for you. You coming back?" I said.

"Nah, we just wanted you to flush all that shit down the toilet," they said.

You motherfuckers, I thought.

I loved the idea of making a lot of money in the weed business. I saw those guys on the beach—my peers—driving Cadillacs, getting girls, partying hard, having fun. That's what I wanted to do and what I wanted to be. And that's how it began.

After I had started dealing pretty heavily, going up and down the coast, I had met a guy named Steve Lamb, who was experienced in—how shall we say it—higher stakes in the drug business. Steve was a legend, and there was a lot you couldn't explain about Steve. He even had a dog that could add, subtract, multiply, and divide on voice command. Steve was part of the crowd on the beach, part of a group that called themselves SBG—South Beach Guys, a group from Pass-a-Grille, Florida, which sits at the very end of St. Pete Beach, where all the rich kids lived. He had smuggled, and the police had their eyes on him. I don't know how he figured out how to go to Jamaica and bring back the weed, but he figured it out.

"Steve, I really want to smuggle," I told him.

"Come back here," he said, and he led me back to his bedroom, and he gave me a souvenir.

"You hang onto this thing," he said, "and you'll have a smuggle."

I did, and I did.

The souvenir: A sea bean.

It was a mystical souvenir from a mystical guy.

I held onto that good luck charm, and eventually my turn came.

CHAPTER 7

GUYS, PUT YOUR GUNS AWAY! IT'S ONLY MARIJUANA

Summers could be slow, as there was no Jamaican or Colombian weed coming into the U.S. because of their harvest schedule. During the time I really started selling, we got word that there were thousands of acres of weed growing wild along the banks of Missouri River. It was hemp. Over the years, floods had carried the hemp seeds down the river, and in the summertime, there was just tons of weed growing. The first summer, I got two Chevy Impalas with huge trunks, put three guys in each car, and drove to St. Joseph, Missouri, to harvest the weed.

We'd start early in the morning in the broad daylight next to a farmer's field, walk along a creek bank, and pull weed off the plants. We were out there sweating our asses off, stuffing our bags full of weed until sundown. Then we'd go up to the flood levees and pull pot from there. We did that trip—Florida to Missouri, pulling weed, back to Florida—in 72 hours. When we got back to a camp site near the Itchetucknee River in north Florida, we'd lay out big sheets and dry the pot out.

We had a contact who would pay 50 bucks a pound for this Missouri River funk weed, so I had a sale waiting. For that weekend's work, I'd pay $1,000, and I'd keep $4,000 or $5,000.

One of my neighbors from the beach was from Rochester, and he told me he could get 300 bucks a pound for this. Well, shit. I was thinking, let's fill up a foot locker and bring it to New York. We did that, but they ended up being pissed at how bad the weed was (and I had to make up for it by bringing them good weed). That's how my Rochester connection started.

I knew what I was working toward—smuggling—but I knew that in order to get into the business, you had to be a stand-up guy: If you got busted, you couldn't take anyone else to jail with you. Do your time, don't bring anyone else down with you. A rite of passage in the business. An accepted social contract. An illegal business built on a foundation of trust.

That was the most important thing. And that's a hell of a funny thing when you think about it. Fucking ironic, right?

I moved fast, and I learned to do as much as I could in the business. I was selling a lot, and I was driving up and down the east coast. One of my main stops was New York. Connie and I—now married—would line a camper van with weed, cover it with camping equipment, and drive up I-95 to Rochester selling weed along the way to people we knew. I met a lot of good people up in New York—a lot of community college students who bought. That's how it worked: We met people, we sold, we expanded our business to wherever there was a demand.

We ran the weed up and down the coast, and we stayed for long stretches of time in New York. And that's where I learned how some of the soldiers smuggled pot back from Vietnam.

I learned a real important lesson there: People want *good* weed, not that shit where you get a headache and don't get high. When you try to sell shit, you get burned, you lose your credibility, and your business won't work. I knew good weed when I saw it, smelled it, and smoked it—it was that Colombian and Jamaican weed that we'd have on St. Pete Beach.

With my Rochester connection, I developed a system. I had three guys bring me the weed in a pickup truck. They'd pick the weed, dry it, and bring it to me in New York. In 1973, I had been storing several hundred pounds in a house in Rochester.

One day, I had a deal, and I felt—in my gut—it was shaky. I met the guys I had a deal with at a bar, and the DEA had spotters out at the bar. They saw us, we saw them, so we knew it. I kept pressuring my guy and asking if he was a cop or an informant, and he kept saying he wasn't. It didn't feel right, but at this point, we needed money, so we went ahead with the deal.

So we met at a bar on one side of Rochester. We got in the guy's car and drove to the woods where I stored four bales of weed—over a hundred pounds—in the woods in a little town of Webster, New York, which was nestled between Rochester and Lake Ontario.

Through the woods, maybe a few hundred feet away, we could see the Webster Police Department. We were so close that you could see cars coming in and out of the department, but they couldn't see anybody through the thick trees.

When we pulled into the woods, I got out and started dragging the bales of weed to the car.

All of a sudden, cop cars started streaming in behind us. It was the DEA. Seven of them.

Damn. I knew it didn't feel right.

And here I am, out there in my tank top, flip flops, and straw hat.

I looked about as threatening as a newborn pussy cat, and they were acting like I wanted to fucking overthrow a monarchy or some shit like that.

Immediately, all seven of the DEA agents surrounded me and drew their guns.

"Guys, it's only marijuana. Jesus Christ! Put your guns away," I yelled.

By this time, the Webster PD was going in for a shift change. They drove by, saw all these clowns with their guns drawn and pulled in behind them. Now they drew their guns. Jesus.

Cops pointing guns at cops, and I'm sitting there with a hundred pounds of weed.

I said it to them again, "Put the fucking guns away. It's only weed!"

After they took me in, I was sitting in the police department—nobody had arrested me, nobody had said anything to me—and I launched into this really wild tale about where the pot had come from.

I was a farmer from Indiana, I said (I still had an Indiana driver's license), and I grew this weed on my farm.

"You're being awful talkative," one of the cops said. "Why are you talking so much?"

"Nobody's read me my rights," I said, "so I'm just here talking."

I was lying like a motherfucker, and they huddled and decided to finally arrest me. This was the first time I had ever been arrested in my life—not even a speeding ticket for me, though God knows I did a bunch of shit to deserve to be arrested by this point. For all they knew, I was a good Christian boy from Indiana. They eventually took me to Buffalo, and I sat in an Erie County jail for five days while I got bond money. They then transported me to Rochester, where they shaved my hippie long hair and cut off my hippie long beard. When Connie picked me up, she didn't even recognize me because she had never seen me without my beard.

So I waited there for my trial, staying up there the entire winter of 1973. Instead of Cold as Fuck, Indiana, I had relocated to Cold as Fuck, New York.

One time during this stretch, I was at a bar with a buddy of mine—we were eating valiums and drinking all day long. I started playing pool, and I could not lose. I mean, I was fucking winning everything like I was on the total zone. We were playing for drinks, naturally, so I kept getting drinks bought for me. And I just racked them up—must have been a dozen or so. Nobody could beat me. At one point, Connie walked into the bar, because she must have been tired of waiting for me. We lived about a mile away.

"Are you coming home?" she said.

"Yeah, I'm coming home, but I gotta lose and I gotta drink all these drinks before I come home," I said.

"Ok," she said.

When I got ready to leave, I saw that my coat was missing. Connie took my fucking coat and my van and left me a mile from home in 20-degree weather. So I had to fucking walk.

I was furious.

When I got home, she came down the stairs. "Hahahahaha, motherfucker," she taunted me in my face.

BOOOOOOOOM!

I nailed her dead right in the fucking nose.

That was the first time I ever hit a woman in my life.

It was stupid, and I regretted it, for sure. But I was pissed. And drunk. And high.

That shit never goes away. She took pictures of her black eyes and flattened-out nose, but she didn't pursue charges or anything like that. We overcame that, and I knew I was wrong—but I was so fucking pissed about what she did.

Awaiting trial during this time, I decided two things.

One, I was not going to give anyone else up. Remember, if I wanted to get into smuggling, I had to prove my worth and I had to be trusted. You snitch, and you're out. So I kept my mouth shut. Two, I decided that this case wasn't just about me. I was going to take on the federal government. I didn't want to beat the charge. I wanted to make a fucking point about the bullshit arrest they made, about how weed should be legal, about the how the government was so fucking stupid about its priorities.

Here's how: These clowns charged me with intent to distribute 107 pounds of cannibas sativa L, and I did not have cannibas sativa L. I had cannibas Americanas—a completely different breed. What I had in the woods? There was no statute on the books saying it was illegal.

After reviewing all of the information, my lawyer decided that this would be a fairly easy case and that I could essentially make it go away by paying a fine. He said, "This is a clear-cut case of entrapment. Five thousand dollars and you can go home."

My lawyer was telling me—just let him fight the charge, show the feds you made a mistake, and you'll get off. He didn't want me to turn this easy case into a federal case, literally.

I told him I didn't care about jail.

"This law is wrong, and I think we have a way to attack the law," I said.

"It's really hard to take on the government. They have all the power," he said.

"I want to do it anyway."

So I went to court over that issue about charging me for a drug that wasn't illegal, according to the law. In federal court in Rochester, my mother and Connie were the only ones sitting in the court room.

My dad learned about it, because my driver's license was from Indiana—so when I got arrested, an item appeared in the local Indiana paper. Talk about an embarrassment to the family. Here I had already brought shame to my family for leaving Kathy, and now I brought more shame to the family after being arrested with 100 pounds of weed. I disappointed a lot of people with the lifestyle I chose. The only thing my dad ever said to me was when he left me a message. "Don't ask me for any help."

I didn't intend to anyway.

My mom, though, just loved me to death. I was the only boy and clearly the favorite (that has to have had an effect on my sisters, for sure).

At trial, the government presented first, and seven DEA agents got on the stand and lied.

Jesus Fucking Christ. Seven cops told the same lie that they had read me rights when they hadn't. How the fuck could they do this? The jury hated the DEA, and they wanted me on the stand to refute that. But I didn't do that. I sacrificed myself to take on the government and testify to the science and the law. We got plant scientists from the University of Illinois to testify about the classifications of the plants, and the jury loved me. The government had no idea I would do that. They thought, for sure, that I would fight them on entrapment—and that's why the DEA lied about reading my rights.

At the end of the trial, in the charge to the jury, the judge gave them the instruction that sealed my fate:

"You have to ignore the defendant's testimony. This is a constitutional question. Constitutional questions cannot be decided at this level of the federal judiciary."

The jury—despite the fact that they loved me—had no choice. They had to find me guilty for selling all that weed.

My sentence: A year and a day in a federal penitentiary, plus three years of special parole. This special parole was designed for drug charges only. It created the recidivism of drug defendants. Example: If I violated at any time, I would return to prison for three years and when I got out, I would still have three years of special parole to do. That sentence would be the one that put me in jail, but also the one that introduced me to the people who would eventually put me on a sailboat to Colombia.

Getting arrested and sentence for selling weed was exactly what led me to living my dream of smuggling it.

CHAPTER 8

MY FIRST SMUGGLE: TUNA AND MAYO

My arrest and sentencing proved to be an important moment for me for a couple reasons: There, I proved to be the standup guy. I didn't name anyone else who could have been implicated and then charged with a crime. I took the arrest myself—and went down for the crime. It's also where my smuggling dreams started to come together.

I came back to Florida while waiting for a decision on my appeal. Before I went to prison, I got a job at Sperry Electronics (the missile system I worked on in the military was Sperry, so they hired me right up—I hadn't told them about my arrest).

Connie and I were both working, and I had moved into a little town off the beach called Hudson, which is little north of Tampa and St. Pete Beach—and away from all the people I had worked with.

Connie had been working at a golf club in Tarpon Springs, and I had a shitty job waiting for trial.

When I lost the appeal in November 1975, I had run out of money. I wanted to go to Supreme Court with this, but I couldn't come up with the money to pay all the legal fees that it would take to do so.

In January 1976, I turned myself in, thinking I would go to Eglin Air Force Base, a minimum-security facility. I was in Hillsborough County jail for five days when two U.S. marshals picked me up.

"We're going to Eglin, right?" I said.

"No, we're going to New York City," one replied.

"Why are you doing that? I thought the feds tried to keep you close to home."

They said that the feds had my home listed as New York, so they were sending me to a facility up north.

When we arrived in New York, we got to a detention facility—nothing more than cages really and a mass of humanity. The guy looked at my papers and said, "What the fuck are we going to do with you? We never have minimum-security people in this place."

Fuck. That didn't seem like a good thing.

Right away, they gave me a job. It was loading supplies from the warehouse into carts and taking it back inside. In the mornings, I'd start in the garbage dumps—killing big fucking rats out there.

One day, a guy there came up to me and said, "You know, you've got a really powerful job. You have access to things that nobody else has access to. We got people in here who can't get socks and underwear. You think you can get that?"

So I asked around and my guard told me, "I don't care what you bring in, but if you get caught, don't bring it back on me."

Fair enough, I thought.

Every shift, I was stuffing my coat pockets full of the goods they wanted. In return, they gave me a series of codes I could use to call my wife in Florida as many times as I wanted to (using FBI switchboard codes, which were obtained by the Italian guys in prison). That was a good trade, I figured. I bring them socks, underwear, tuna, and mayonnaise, and I got to call Connie.

It took two weeks to get the paperwork to send me back to Eglin. Finally, we left on a prison bus. On the bus, there was a guy there named Tony. Big guy, didn't know how to act. I could see he was going to get hurt really bad by some of the bad dudes on the bus. Well, he got into it with them, and I intervened and broke it up and looked after him on the rest of the bus trip. We ended up in Atlanta federal pen—a real bad place in terms of violence. It had a reputation of being the worst of the worst. But I had helped Tony, so that apparently had some benefits. At about 3 o'clock in the morning, a guy showed up outside of my jail cell and said, "You want a steak? I got a T-bone steak and a baked potato. Thanks for taking care of Tony."

I didn't know who the fuck Tony was or why he was important, but here I was getting fed a T-bone steak in the scariest prison the country.

I also met a guy named Blue. I soon learned why they called him that. He was so black he was blue. Blue had been locked up in solitary for 14 years of life, and he was famous in the prison system. I had a good rapport with him, sitting in the rec yard shooting shit about philosophy and life. Baddest dude in prison and we were friends. Meeting people and doing right by them leads to good things.

We were in Atlanta for two weeks before the bus came to take us to Eglin.

It was a minimum-security work camp, so we all had jobs. But it was about as low-key as it gets, as far as prison was concerned.

It was just a place with white-collar criminals, lawyers, politicians, Watergate burlglars, pot people, inmates like that. Still I got a real sense of what it's like to live in totalitarian state—you gotta do what you're told, do your work, stay in line. The food wasn't all that bad (it wasn't that good either). I did a lot of work, a lot of reading, and a ton of exercising (I did 1,000 reps of abs exercises twice a fucking day). Once, the prison asked me to participate in some July 4 competition or some shit like that. I told them no fucking way. I'm not doing anything for you. I'm not giving you one lick of satisfaction that I'm enjoying this. I'm getting in the shape of my life for me, not you. I refused to participate in their organized athletics. I was obstinate. You're taking my freedom away; I'm not doing shit for you.

We did smoke weed nearly every day in prison. We'd take turns rolling the joints, and sometimes we'd even run into some really good stuff. One of us had to hold the camp stash every day—rolling 21 joints a day. We'd even drink in the warehouse in between our work details—beer during the day and we had martinis with some Jewish lawyer at night (remember, this is minimum security).

One day after work, we were in the yard, and I threw a long football pass to another guy. And my arm just instantly went ice cold— strangest sensation in the world, felt frozen solid. After a few hours, the feeling came back, but I noticed over the next few days, that my hands were shrinking and my fingers were wrinkling. The doctor sent me to the base hospital because there was nothing the prison doc could do. They found that I had collapsed my carpal tunnel nerve, so I couldn't work because they had to do surgery.

During that time, that's when the U.S. evacuated Vietnam. And they gave inmates extra benefits if we would work at night to build tent cities for all the Vietnamese who would arriving. Because I was on non-work status because of my injury, I couldn't get on the details. The inmates who were working quickly discovered that the Vietnamese coming in had duffel bags of Thai Stick—really high-quality Thai weed with the most beautiful buds in the world wrapped around a stick. I had only read about these in High Times magazine.

The prison didn't really know what to do with me because of my injury: I'm in a work camp, and I can't fucking work.

So I'm bored to death and go to the grounds chief.

"You got anything I can do?"

He gave me a stick with a nail to pick up trash around the grounds. That sounded good to me. I just needed to do something. That was my job.

I walked the track—three-quarters a mile around the perimeter—and inmates started coming to me.

"You think you could bring something in for me?" they asked.

"Like what?" I said.

They wanted real food—food they could smuggle in for the weekends. I got them food, and they paid me in weed.

Something else happened because of my job picking up trash: I was the first person that E. Howard Hunt saw when he pulled up to camp in his black limousine. Hunt, of course, was the former CIA officer who was charged with burglary, conspiracy, and wiretapping in the Watergate scandal. During his orientation at Eglin, he seemed to take a liking to the work I was doing, since I got to go places where no other inmates could go.

"From what I can tell," he told me, "you've got the best job on the compound. How much do you want for it?"

"It's not for sale," I said.

"Everything's for sale," he replied. "How much do you want?"

Ha. This was a former CIA agent wanting to buy me off. I told him it was a volunteer job and that he could ask the grounds chief if he could do it, but it wasn't something he could buy. It was probably the first time in his life he couldn't just use money to get what he wanted.

We talked a few times, and he was such a smart guy. I enjoyed our conversations. When he was assigned a bunk, it was next to one of my homies, Dude, and he had hidden our group's weed stash in the empty mattress. So once Howard moved into that bed, we couldn't get to our weed for a week until laundry day. (I was also amused to hear that a few other Watergate burglars were at Eglin with us and when the door was locked to the parole room before their hearing and guards were looking for the keys, those guys just went ahead and picked the lock to get in.)

I had started to run on the track and built up to running about 9 miles at a time. (I came out of there with a great tan and in great shape—I was down to a lean 130 pounds.)

One time, an older, white gentleman came up to me and asked if he could run with me.

"You can, but you gotta keep up. I'm not slowing down," I said, because it didn't look like he could run real well.

His name was Tommy. He had an in with an inmate who had access to a fridge in the camp dentist office, so we got to eat ice cream every night. Tommy was a white-collar criminal, and I was intrigued by robbing banks and other types of white-collar crime he did. We became friends.

I was in prison with a short-term sentence, and nobody ever made parole. So when it was my turn to go up to the parole board after about three months, I didn't have a lot of optimism and I didn't give too much of a fuck anyway. The time served for a year sentence was about eight months, but you'd meet with the parole board at the three-month mark.

I had letters from my electronics shop, my wife, lots of people, even the sentencing judge because he knew the whole fucking arrest was bullshit. But it didn't matter. These parole people were the coldest motherfuckers there were. They didn't give a shit. They practically had DENIED tattooed on their foreheads.

So when it was my turn, I reported to the three members of the board who were there and would decide my fate. One asked, "What makes you think you deserve to get out on parole?"

"Do you have all the information sent to you?" I responded, referring to all my letters of support.

"Yes, we have that."

"Then I've got nothing else to say."

Boom. Fuck you. I'm not justifying my shit to you motherfuckers, I thought. With nothing to lose, I walked out of the room.

The next posting of parole was soon posted on the bulletin board: Fuck if I didn't make parole at a time when nobody did, and I was scheduled to get out in six months on a sentence of a year and a day.

CHAPTER 9

CAN YOU SAIL TO THE MOTHERSHIP?

When I was released from prison, things were good, but I had to do six months of parole and then another three-year phase of special parole after that, and that was a motherfucker pain in the ass. My drinking started getting out of control, even though I had my electronics job and was working on a cool project. During this time, the IRS started sending me letters saying I owed $10,000. They agreed that I could pay them $50 a month until we figured it out. It was a mess. The revenue agent said I could pay or go fishing. I had to quit my great electronics job because the IRS put a lien on my wages until it was settled. I had dabbled in the restaurant and bar business and had thought that if I could back get into that, I could do what I really wanted to do—finance a boat and get into the fishing business

I opened a bar and restaurant in Tarpon Springs, where Connie had found a place—working 12 to 14 hours a day trying to make it a success. Tarpon Springs was another coastal town along the Gulf Mexico, and it's especially known for its Greek population—highest percentage of Greek Americans of any U.S. city, in fact. Not surprisingly, it was named that because some early settlers saw some tarpon jumping out of the water there.

My drinking was getting worse and worse. I was out all the time, drinking all the time. Though I had the restaurant in the black in seven months, I knew I didn't belong in the restaurant business in a Greek town. I was—like the name of the actual town—a fish out of water.

It took some time, but I figured out that the way to get into the fishing business wasn't by being in the bar business. You had to fish to get into fishing.

After seven months in a bar, I knew that I didn't have it to make my life work serving sandwiches and pints, but I did have an opportunity. I was living in a fishing town, so I decided to see a captain of a fishing boat and learn the sea.

I made two trips with a guy named Captain Slim in the Super Snapper. He told me he had never taken anyone to sea who paid attention as well I did and who learned as well as I did.

"Gary, there's only one job on this boat and you can't have it, and it's mine. You gotta go somewhere else," he said.

So I got a job on a 65-foot shrimp trawler that was being converted to a fishing boat. We redid everything and got it ready to go to sea. They wanted to take it to Charleston, South Carolina. So four or five of us took it down from Tarpon Springs to Fort Myers (which was further south on the west coast), cut across Florida to the intercoastal waterway, up to St. Augustine to head to the Atlantic and up to Charleston.

Only problem: Nobody fucking knew how to navigate.

The captain didn't really want to do this; he preferred his quart and a half of rum a day.

Now, make no mistake, he knew the sea. After all, he was a former Coast Guard, a high-line fisherman, bringing 60,000 of pounds red snapper back to sell. All his skills were with a sextant, and he didn't know how to navigate with electronic Loran. So I read up on it, learned the system, and became first mate.

I got us right on point to Charleston, and that was a huge win. My navigation skills were on point, and I proved to be a valuable part of the crew. But we had a problem.

The boat was fucking leaking—it was built the same year I was born in: 1946.

So when we got to Schimm Creek, where the shrimp boats docked in Charleston, we had to crank this thing up to fix the leak. We got it way up off the ground, so we were pretty high up and had a great view all around us.

One of the mates had binoculars.

"Gary," he said, "there's a girl on that sailboat over there."

"Really?"

I walked over there and started hollering at her. She considered herself a sailboat bum, living out on an old dry-dock sailboat. It turned out, though, that Sam was a trust-fund baby, and she was from a big banking family living in a dry-dock sailboat. She was smart, though a little homely, but she had a lot of money. Any port in the storm, right?

Sam joined us and our crew, and we became a thing, making those runs from Florida to Charleston. Every time we docked in South Carolina, we'd check in to the nice Hilton in Charleston and spend three or four nights there while the rest of the guys were on the boat. We had a great time, great sex, great fun, great weed.

She presented herself as a purist in sailing, so we actually hired her to be a cook on the boat, even though she couldn't cook. She couldn't fucking do it. At all. She couldn't even cook eggs on the trawler because she didn't have the sea legs to stand up as the boat rocked. Now, I'll cut her a little slack because shrimp trawlers are round-bottom boats (they're designed that way so they don't catch the fishing nets when they turn), but that means those suckers will rock and roll unless they have stabilizing outriggers. My fucking captain took off the outriggers, so this trawler really had us off-balance. You had to work hard to stay upright. Sam just couldn't scramble the eggs because she was rocking so much. I said, fuck it, I'll do the cooking. Sam was part of the crew, but not really.

But I got a great blow job every morning, so who the fuck cares if she can scramble some eggs. On those boats, you had time to basically work and fuck and that was it. Sam made four trips with us in all, and we had a nice little relationship.

We also did have some time to smoke every day too. The captain would say, "That's some stinky-ass tobacco." I lied and told him it was Cuban tobacco, and he had no idea it was pot.

When we headed back to Florida on our final trip together, Sam told me she wanted to go to some sailing races going on in Newport, Rhode Island. I told her I'd drive up with her, and I told my Connie we were getting divorced.

About 100 miles into the drive, when we got to Ocala—a small town in north central Florida known for being one of the horse capitals of the country—I decided I didn't want to go to Newport after all. So I told Sam that I didn't want to keep spending her money, and that I wanted to make money on my own. I told her I had friends I had from Eglin that I wanted to see about making money.

"Well, can I go with you?" Sam said.

I said sure, so we headed down to Pompano Beach, which was between Fort Lauderdale and Boca Raton on the east side of Florida along the Atlantic Ocean. There, we got an apartment, and I had one goal: I wanted to see my buddy I met in prison—the guy who followed me on the track, Tommy, a career conman.

I wanted to learn about white-collar crime. When I met up with him, I bullshitted around with Tommy and his partners, and they were fascinated with my sailing experience and time on the sea. Pretty cool story, they thought. I had reinvented myself, living the life on the water, fishing and fucking and finding happiness in the simple joys of exploration and entrepreneurship. Just as you'd imagine, I had gained some skills along the way.

Tommy's partner was a defrocked lawyer named John and a big-time criminal. John was the principal in a master marijuana plan that I was soon to get involved in. He was the point person, the guy who ran it all. John was a short little Jewish fellow who wore a toupee all the time. When he wasn't wearing it, his head looked like a penis, and he was real insecure about it. He was the kingpin—drove Cadillacs and Rolls Royces, had nice houses and nice women, toupee and all. He was even with a beauty queen, a Miss Texas, if I remember right. I asked him how much all of this cost.

"You can't afford it," he said.

So I just stole his fucking woman. She wouldn't fuck him anyway, so I stole her.

Tommy and John had made their money essentially finding crooked bank presidents and getting them to liquidate some of the bank's holdings—and then paying them a hefty fee for doing so.

The two of them worked with John's brother, Bobbi. Bobbi turned out to be a fucking MVP when it came to pulling off the big smuggle from Colombia. Bobbi, like the others, was a brilliant guy. He was laid back, which made him perfect to handle some of the high-pressure situations we would find ourselves in. Bobbi negotiated that his portion of the upcoming adventure wouldn't be cash—but he'd get the boat, a beautiful 47-foot sailboat that ended up getting beat to shit on our journey. But it was a good haul in any case, since it probably was a quarter-million-dollar vessel. A guy named Cool Hand Sevi was also their friend and part of the inner circle. Nice enough guy who owned a condo in Pompano and who would end up helping out a lot on the smuggle.

When I met with John and Tommy, they were intrigued by my drug-dealing background, and they were also interested in my time on boats. Hell, I wanted to learn about their bank crimes. I had no idea that our conversation would go in the direction that it did.

"You know the sea?" John said.

"Yeah, I can navigate. I've sailed little boats."

"Do you think you could take a sailboat out to a mothership to load 9,000 pounds of pot on it?" John said.

The trip would be a couple hours tops.

Fucking famous last words.

I'm sure my response sounded cocky as fuck, but inside, I'm thinking, holy fuck. This is it. Could I really do this? Pull off a real smuggle? With big-time drugs? Holy shit.

"Yeah, I can do that," I said.

I wanted to learn new crime, and they wanted to learn new crime—they didn't want to rob banks anymore. And drug smuggling seemed like a fine way to make a lot of money. So they told me to go ahead and hire a crew for the trip. They showed me the boat, and it was a beautiful sailboat—nearly 50 feet long—that looked like a luxury yacht.

I went back to St. Pete Beach, where all my friends were, and I hired two crew members. I offered each one of the guys $30,000, and John offered me a percentage of the load—which, I calculated, would equate to about a thousand pounds.

What was supposed to last a couple days turned out to be much longer and what was supposed to be a thousand pounds turned out to be much more.

CHAPTER 10

YOU CAN'T SAIL?

Before we did the big smuggle, we had to orchestrate some plane smuggles on a Cessna 310 from West Palm Beach. We were to take the plane to Colombia and load with weed. My pilot Johnny had been a chopper pilot in Vietnam War. He had a CIA passport so he had free clearance to fly to Colombia. After we took off to Colombia, the plane shut down near the Bahamas.

Something with the fuel line was fucked up. We went from 5,000 feet to 500 feet, but finally the fuel kicked in and we were able to land in Andros Island. We finally got a hold of someone in customs and told them we needed someone to check us in.

"Today? Everybody's drunk. It's like our Fourth of July," the guy on the other end of the line said.

The custom guy came out, drunk, and Johnny—a hot-headed Italian—had a little friction with the guys. I stepped in, made nice, and we ended up partying with them. When we flew back without the pot, we had customs all over us again. The next time they tried to smuggle, I wasn't involved in the plane part of it, but was on the ground crew. They brought a 3,500-pound stash back and guys were unloading it off a trailer park. We had a police scanner, and we knew they were on the way. We had good intel. We put the guys in a Cadillac and sent them away, but the vans went the other direction. The people at the trailer park told them to look for a white Cadillac, so while they were chasing the Cadillac, the vans were gone—the were painted and the weed was distributed before the cops would get any clue.

This smuggle got the drugs that would finance the big boat smuggle to the mothership off of Colombia.

Before I left for Colombia—even though I had sailed, this fucking adventure felt way out my league, though I was cocky enough that it didn't bother me—I came to a pretty simple conclusion: What's the worst thing that happen to me? One, I could go to jail. Two, I could die. The best thing? I could succeed.

Well, I've been to jail so that didn't bother me, and what the fuck, everybody's going to die anyway, so that hasn't been much of a fear factor to me. So I might as well live my dream.

I would be taking two guys with me to Colombia—black Johnny and red Woody (there were a couple guys named Woody, so this was red-headed Woody). I was ditching my wife, but Johnny and Woody needed a few days to get their stuff together, say goodbye to their wives, and prepare for our cross-state trip from St. Pete Beach to Pompano Beach, where the sailboat waited. Johnny was a short, stocky guy. Wild too. Almost died a couple times in drunk-driving wrecks. Woody was just one of the guys in the beach, normal enough guy ready for a big payday after the smuggle.

That boat was spectacular—a 47-foot-long, 24-foot-wide sailboat with two massive masts and a fuckload of different sails packed to handle all kinds of wind conditions.

Sam, the woman I met in Charleston, knew how to sail, or so she bragged, and I needed a good sailor, because I didn't know shit about sailing big boats. I could navigate, yes, but sail? No. That's why I invited her to be part of the crew. As we were driving up the highway in a big-ass, white 1969 El Dorado convertible after showing my friends and Sam the boat, Sam had a confession, or the way she put it: She had to clarify something.

"All I really know about sailing is steering the boat," Sam said.

"All these fucking months, you've been giving me shit and you don't know how to fucking sail?" I yelled. I fucking lost it. I was depending on her, and now she tells me all she can do is hold a fucking wheel. Jesus.

I stopped the car in the middle of the highway, let her out, and that was that. I left her in the middle of the street. I'm a straight shooter, and I was pissed. Don't blow smoke up my ass about what you can and can't do. I didn't need liars. I needed a crew.

Never saw her again.

We spent three weeks in Pompano Beach getting the boat ready for the journey that would take us more than 1,000 miles from Florida to Colombia, though little did we know that we'd be forced to make it go almost 2,000 miles out of our way to evade the feds. The vessel had a nice name, but fuck if I can remember what it was because I changed the name of it every single time I called shore.

During our prep time, we discussed schedules, radio codes, navigation information. We prepped our communications, which we did through illegal, single-side band radios. We had one radio in the boat and one in an electronics shop next door to a bar in Pompano, which wasn't great because the high-powered energy would crank up the neon lights in the bar, so the cops always wondered what those middle-of-the-night light-ups were all about. We were planning to do twice-a-day calls to check in—always at rotating hours so they never were at the same time. That let us handle any problems at sea, and they could take care of them on land. Communications were the most important part of our prep.

Bobbi's wife, Cheryl, was in charge of the provisions, and she stocked that boat full of everything we needed. We lived off canned meats and canned everything really, and we had a full galley with a fridge and stove. No booze. You gotta be sober when you sail.

We celebrated Thanksgiving 1978 at Bobbi's house. Cheryl made a traditional dinner with ham and turkey. My crew was there with Bobbi's family, and we spent the meal talking about the trip. It was a family affair, for sure. Unorganized crime at its finest.

We would set sail at the crack of dawn the next day.

CHAPTER 11

U.S. NAVY ON OUR TAIL

Our boat was tied up to a private dock behind a friend's aunt's house on the Intercoastal Waterway. That, as you can figure out the name, is a 3,000-mile inland waterway that runs from Massachusetts to the southern part of Florida and up to Texas, using inlets, rivers, sounds, bays, waterways like that.

I was pretty excited when we left at sun up and headed down the Intercoastal Waterway before getting to the Atlantic. I didn't know how to sail, but I knew propulsion systems and I knew how to navigate, so I figured I could learn the rest along the way. It was going to be a short trip after all. Or so I thought.

John and Bobbi were both there when we left.

There was no grand goodbye, just a thumbs up. They had confidence in me, which was pretty surprising, considering that I had never done this before, and they didn't know me for shit. But like I said, there's a lot of trust that goes on in this business, and they were showing it to me. You know, I look back on that time, and it makes me realize this: It's amazing what you can do when you get a small group of ballsy people together. I mean, seriously, you put a core group together, make a plan, and follow through? You can succeed in just about anything. Good life lesson, if you ask me.

Leaving Pompano Beach, we headed south, stopped one night on an island, sailing toward Eleuthera in the Bahamas, cruising through Eleuthera Sound.

The first day of the sail was pretty uneventful. We sailed until sunset to a protected harbor. The crew decided to go on a little island tour in the Bahamas and party a bit. Johnny got himself into a little trouble that night, picking up a woman, taking her back to her house, messing around, and then having to jump out of her window and get back to the boat when the man of the house came home. The first fucking night.

Before we left, the chief of police on that island came to the dock. The people there liked the big, fancy boats that could come to shore.

He came aboard, looked at the boat, and saw our intricate communications system in the cockpit.

"You got some comms," he said. "Why so much?"

I quipped back, "I want to be able to talk to God if I need some help."

I was only half-joking.

On the second day of the trip, I saw in the charts a sea anchor, but it didn't mean much. Over the next couple hours, I thought we were sailing forward, but I noticed that the ship that we saw in the distance was getting closer and closer and closer, and I thought, *What the hell?* I went back and looked at the stern of the boat and saw that we had caught their anchor line—called a hawzer—in our rudder. I felt like I was going forward, but I was sliding up their line and not going anywhere. I didn't know what that boat was, but I called it up on a ship-to-ship line.

It was a U.S. Navy vessel.

"We got a problem here. I've got your hawzer hooked in my rudder, and the only way we're going to get this thing off is if you turn the bow of your ship into the anchor line and get some slack so we can get it out from under there."

"The captain doesn't want to start the boat up," the guy on the other end of the radio said.

"Then I'll have to cut the line," I replied.

So they sent two small boats out to take a look, which they did, and then reported back that if they didn't turn the boat, there'd be a disaster. So the captain started it up and they fixed the problem. And we were both on our way.

It wasn't really a close call—especially because we didn't have anything on board yet—but it felt like a semi-close call. We really didn't need any meetups with the U.S. military when our goal was to get thousands of pounds of marijuana on board very soon.

We sailed all night and then pulled into a port to prepare to head to the Windward Passage—a straight in the Caribbean Sea—toward Colombia. When we got ready to leave, somebody at the dock told us not to leave at that time of the day because the current through the island country of Turks and Caicos (which is made up of about 100 islands) were too strong and we wouldn't make it unless we left early in the morning. I tried it anyway and blew out our autopilot system, so we headed back to port. Bobbi flew down to get a new system.

After that was fixed, we left early in the morning and winded our way between Haiti and Cuba. There's no wind between the mountains, so you have to motor through. And that's when we started ripping out all the furniture in the boat—tables, beds, all of it—to toss it overboard and make room in the boat for all the pot. I sometimes think about those fucking beds sitting there at the bottom of Atlantic somewhere—a sea-residing souvenir of a long-ago pot smuggle.

As we were coming around the edge of Haiti, local fishermen were holding up beautiful red snappers and lobster. They started paddling toward the boat wanting to sell us fish. As much as I wanted it, I said no way am I letting them near my boat. There was a ton of pirating going on, and these guys are fucking Haitians. They could be getting ready to hijack our boat and take us to Miami. So we motored past them and hit the open waters of the Caribbean.

There's always something to do on the boat, always something to pay attention to—you don't take a minute off when you're sailing. And when you consider that my two crew guys had no sailing experience, we really had to work—and I had to do a lot of teaching. If we didn't pay close attention, we'd be totally fucked—lost in the Caribbean with no navigation aids or anything.

In the winter, the wind comes out of the east and with the 30 mph winds, I had that boat going over 25 knots—about 28 mph—on sail power alone. A gorgeous ride. Mild and gentle seas. We were screaming across the Caribbean and because of that, we got to the coast of Colombia 12 hours ahead of schedule—just three or four days after we left Florida.

When we hit the coast, I had to motor along the coast, just taking in the weather, the scenery, the majesty of it all. The dolphins would come up, play around the boat, ride in the wake, trying to catch a ride. It was fucking beautiful.

The people we were supposed to meet for the pot dropoff sent a plane out to find us, then they flew low to drop a milk bottle in the ocean that contained the coordinates of where we would meet to pick up the pot. That was our technology at the time. A fucking milk bottle.

The first time they tried, the bottle sank.

So they had to send out another one, and we got that one.

CHAPTER 12

THE DROP OFF

When we got to the rendezvous point at about 9 or 10 at night, it was pitch black. The Colombians had to use fire on sticks for their light, so we could see them as they started coming up to us in dozens of little dugout canoes—real narrow things, fisherman boats.

They had bales of marijuana stacked 9-feet high in them. I had no idea how they didn't tip over. Amazing.

When they got to us—boat after boat after boat—they took those bales off and loaded them up on ours. Stacks and stacks of weed. It took a good two or three hours to load the boat.

They also brought 50-gallon drums of diesel, so I had enough fuel if I needed it. There's no money exchange at this point; that all happens later. We just had to give them human collateral in advance. We had this old guy named Eddie, who served as our hostage. He was flown to Colombia to be the collateral. Our principal, John, was there on the little boats, and Eddie was the hostage until we got back with the pot.

Eddie got paid to be the hostage (and would be safely returned when it was all over), but two years later, he got shot in a bar in Fort Lauderdale. Someone just walked in and blew him away. We found out because we had a guy we worked with who called us and said Eddie had been shot. And our guy was freaked out.

"Gary, the boys who killed Eddie are sitting inside my motel room. What do I do?"

We all huddled and told him, "Do exactly what I say and do it right fucking now. Walk out of the motel. Somebody will pick you up in 5 minutes." He did, and a crew picked up our guy.

Damn, that's how it worked to protect your people.

I debated hiring a hit man to kill the guy who killed Eddie, but after I met with the guy, I reconsidered.

"I'll do it no problem," the hit man told me. "But the thing you have to keep in mind if that if this ever falls down, it will never fall down on me."

Meaning, if he gets caught, I'm the one going down for it.

I called off the hit and that was that. That was the closest I ever came to doing something illegal besides drugs, and I wanted no part of the violent aspect of this world. Never did, never have, and never will. No drugs are worth killing over. And that's a big reason why the drug business is so fucked up today, because of all the violence associated with it.

On the boat after the loading of the five-plus tons of marijuana, the group of indigenous people finished up and presented us with a gift: A slaughtered and skinned goat that we could use for meat on our return trip.

What the fuck am I going to do with a goat?

We didn't have a fridge big enough to store it, so we ended up dumping it soon after we left, but the only problem was that nobody fucking told me that we were supposed to give them a gift too. Well, we didn't have shit on the boat, except the two guns I kept to protect ourselves in case we were hijacked, and they sure as shit weren't getting them.

But they weren't leaving without a gift, so they took the canvas door off of the captain's wheelhouse and kept that as a souvenir. I didn't think it was that big of a deal at the time, though it would turn out to be more of a problem than I could have imagined.

The exchange happened on Christmas Eve 1978. The load was supposed to total 9,000 pounds, but it turned out to be 11,000 pounds. These bales took up every bit of room in the pontoons of the boat. They were stacked six or so feet high wrapped all over in canvas (we ended up sleeping on them because we had thrown out our beds on the way down). Our team would be paying $15 a pound for it, so it was quite a valuable stash of hash. The math: They would pay about $165,000 for it—and then, of course, they'd sell it for thousands and thousands more than that.

That night, after we loaded up, we got a radio call from our home base.

"You can't go through the passage you came down through. The Coast Guard threw up a blockade through Fort Lauderdale to Antigua."

We had to detour.

How far out of our way?

Like 1,700 miles east in the Caribbean.

"Holy fuck, that's going to take forever."

But we had to do it, or else we'd risk getting caught with five-and-a-half tons of marijuana on our boat.

When we were told we'd have to navigate around the Coast Guard blockade, we had no choice but to sail way out of the way with hopes of making it back to Florida at some point down the line. If I tried to go the way I came, they said, I would "face imminent arrest." What was supposed to be a trip of about a week was now looking like it would last a whole lot longer than that.

I wasn't scared of jail, but I didn't have any desire to go if I could avoid it.

The day we loaded the weed, we had to head east—and it meant we would have to go toward a place in the sea where my navigation system wouldn't work. That was a problem, but we would learn to manage and learn to figure it out. Actually, I had to figure it out— Johnny and Woody were about as close to useless as you could get when it came to the actual travels.

I didn't know it when I left, but my next sighting of land wouldn't be until five weeks later. It didn't take me long to figure out that this short smuggle was going to take months.

What's fucking amazing is that Cheryl had packed the boat with enough food to last us. It's one of the things I learned in the sea business—you always prepare redundancies. You never knew what could go fucking wrong at sea, and you better have backup. Well, God bless Cheryl, because she provisioned us with enough food to help us survive if something went wrong. And here we were, sure as shit, something did.

To get east, I had run into winds that put us almost at a dead stop—I couldn't fucking get anywhere on sails. The first two days, the wind was blowing so hard that I had to motor. When the winds shifted from the southeast, I rode that to the northeast for as long as it blew. When the wind shifted from the northeast, I rode to the southeast as long as it blew. So I essentially had to zigzag my way across the Caribbean, adding days of time, but using as much wind power as I could. Also, the boat didn't like to cooperate all that much with 11,000 pounds of weed on it. Not as maneuverable as it could be. We were headed to Dominica, an island in the Lesser Antilles. It took five weeks to get from the spot where we loaded to the coast of Dominica.

This, of course, was a problem. I couldn't go any of the routes I knew, and I had to head way far out east to get around it all. During that time, I had no navigation aids, so I had to call ship-to-ship to find out where we were.

They gave me their coordinates, and while we avoided a potential stop by the Coast Guard—thankfully we had ins with the Coast Guard who gave us the tip—this change of plans turned a three-day trip into a five-week journey that almost cost us all 11,000 pounds of our weed, not to mention our lives.

I didn't have a whole lot of sailing experience, so I didn't know how the boat would respond to sailing into the wind, because they gave me a destination that was 1,700 miles to the east to get around the blockade.

I didn't panic, and I wasn't nervous. You just deal second to second when you're sailing. The crew had run out of cigarettes, so they were going crazy without their nicotine, and they had no desire to try the pot on board, so they were freaking a bit about how long the trip was taking.

Three weeks into the voyage across the Caribbean, one of the sails had ripped from the piece that held it to the mast. It flopped down a few feet and the piece with the stainless-steel head was swinging 60-feet high. If we didn't get it fixed, it could take our whole mast, and then we'd be really fucked.

As the captain of the boat, I told them, "One of you two have to take the chair, go up, and fix it."

They both said they weren't going to do it.

Fuck, I never had mutiny before.

I said, "Look, if I go up there and get killed, you're going to die anyway because you don't have a fucking clue about how to sail the boat. You haven't taken it upon yourself to learn a fucking thing I'm doing."

"Well, Captain, that's the risk we're going to take," they said. "We ain't going up."

So I hauled my ass up there, caught the piece after it nearly swung into my head, and secured it. Crisis handled, except that I didn't have that sail anymore, and that made sailing less efficient than it could be—because it was a key piece of the rig.

Because those two guys balked and didn't follow my orders, I broke out the sewing kit, and I had them sew the sail back together. For days, they sewed. They sewed and sewed and sewed. Their fingers bled. They did it, and we put it back up, and it ripped again. So I had them sew again. They were so pissed. We had to put together a makeshift sail, and we limped into Dominica.

To get there, I looked at my charts trying to coordinate where we were, and damn if I didn't hit the leeward Dominica right on the button. No motor, no sail. The locals saw me. I could see them. Two or three boats headed out to see if I needed help.

"I need to get in and do some repairs. I need an injector pump, and I need sails," I said. "How's your customs here?"

They told me that if I went to the customs dock, they're going to come on the boat, but they wouldn't if I didn't go to the customs dock. "They're too lazy," they said.

"Take me as far from the customs dock as you can," I said.

Bobbi flew to Dominica to help fix the sails and install a new injector pump so we could get back on our way to get around the Coast Guard blockade. We hired locals to help us with the services we needed, and we got mechanics and all of the stuff we needed. We were staying in a guest house in Portsmouth Harbor. The average income for a Dominican at the time was $600 a year, and these poor people saved pennies all year long just to celebrate carnival, and I'm selling them pot cheap. They're thrilled. Every morning, we'd have breakfast at the guest house, while locals looked after the boat.

My local helper discovered I had two guns on board—a sub-machine gun and a sawed-off shot gun, 12 gauge. Well, damn, they wanted to buy the guns. I wouldn't sell them, but they knew I had weapons. These people were just so friendly and happy, and the woman making us breakfast would point outside and say, "Which chicken do you want for lunch?" We'd pick out our chickens and go back to the boat. We ended up staying almost a week before the boat could get repaired.

One day, I had brought a bag of weed from the boat to the guest house, and some kids had found it. Now, the locals knew we had weed, and they said we had to get out of there. We had worn out our welcome, and luckily our boat was fixed and we could get going.

We took off early on the morning and headed out into the open Atlantic and turned it north toward Daytona Beach, now six weeks into the trip.

In Dominica, I had sent my original crew home, and I told them that Bobbi and Sevi would finish the trip with me.

CHAPTER 13

YOU'RE ON YOUR OWN

Johnny and Woody were pissed. When I sent them home, they assumed they weren't going to get paid, but I needed them for something big—a small action that was key to making this whole trip work. I needed to write a letter to my parole officer, and it had to be a fucking masterpiece. I needed to lie, I needed to convince her that all was good, and I needed her to think that there was nothing to worry about. Only problem? I was in fucking Dominica, and I was supposed to stay put in Florida.

So I said to the guys, "If you take this letter, go back home, drive to Tarpon Springs, Florida, and put this in a mailbox in Tarpon Springs, Florida, maybe I won't go back to prison and I'll pay you your $30,000 each—just to take that letter back to Tarpon Springs."

That letter, as it turns out, cost me $60,000. Plus the stamp.

My letter was indeed a fucking masterpiece. I was allowed to fish on my parole terms, so I wrote a detailed note concocting a lie about how we were in the Gulf, had mechanical problems, and were stuck. The parole officer got the letter and was so convinced it was factual she called my mother to let her know all was good. But my mother knew the lie I told, because I contacted her from the boat, so she had corroborated it. They never questioned me again, and that saved me from going back to prison when I got back to Florida.

Thank you, Johnny and Woody. You bastards almost cost me my life when you wouldn't fix the sail, but you fixed this situation by dropping my letter in a mailbox.

The day after I sent my crew home, Bobbi, Sevi, and I headed up to the Atlantic. The winds were good, and all was going great. I had to fix a hole in the pontoon that was causing some of the bales of weed to get wet (and that we unfortunately had to throw overboard). After we got that hole sealed, we just spent day after day cruising along.

We were past the Leeward Islands, off the coast of Florida about 600 miles, when we caught the back end of the Great Blizzard of 1978, considered one of the most powerful storms in U.S. history.

That thing had come across the country, causing mud slides in California, snowing like crazy across the U.S., a fucking terrible storm. The storm lasted five days across the U.S.—some parts of Michigan got almost three feet of snow, and about 90 people died during that stretch.

We didn't know it was coming, but as it started getting close, we had a feeling that we were really in for it. That's why we made contact with the U.S. Navy base in Jacksonville to see if they knew about the storm. Their response? We were the only boat within a hundred miles.

"You shouldn't be out there," they radioed back. "You're on your own."

That's a scary fucking feeling. And that's living in the moment. Fuck, I wonder if any of those guys at the Navy base ever wondered what happened to us.

Now, we're in deep water—12,000 feet to the bottom—a long way from Florida.

That storm hit and if we had any chance, we had to turn and go *with* it.

We rode that storm for three days.

It was the most intense experience a human can ever endure.

We were in 100 mph winds, 90-foot seas, and the clouds were an angry purple—like a hard-earned bruise of the sky—that I had never seen before. Those clouds were so violent-looking that it made you want to puke. So much nastiness in the clouds. Rain, lightning, wind, waves.

I learned something important during those three days: I apparently don't have a fear gene. I was reveling in the moment, steering just to keep us alive, and living every second by every second. I had never seen anything like that in my fucking life, and I was just trying to survive, while Mother Nature was just throwing her ugliest at you. It was a supernatural temper tantrum unlike any other.

But I never got afraid. That's how I pretty much live my life anyway—second by second. It's amazing what humans can do when they need to.

I just tried to steer the boat true, slaloming down the waves like a skier or surfer—never going straight down, which would have surely broken the boat into pieces. I had a little sail and the engine running for steering. For three days, I held onto the helm riding this thing out. Remember, the Colombians had taken the door off, so the wind and rain just constantly ripped through me. I had no protection at all from the storm in the wheelhouse.

Bobbi and Sevi? They were fucking scared to death.

Whenever I would get a small lull, I tried to sleep an hour or so. And when I laid down, I just listened to the violence, all while the boat was just working and creaking, and I just wondered if this thing was going to break apart in pieces—and I'd take my rightful place in the bottom-of-the-ocean bed we had thrown overboard at the start of the trip.

"Wake up, wake up, wake up, it's starting back up again," Bobbi and Sevi would say when the weather got more intense.

We had an AM radio going on as much as we could, and at one point in the storm, a Bee Gees song came on, I shit you not.

"Staying Alive."

That's when Bobbi really lost his shit.

"I'm going to die, I'm going to die," he kept saying over and over. He started talking about his wife and kids. He got on the radio and gave his wife our exact location and apologized for everything he'd done, knowing he'd never see her again.

After three long fucking days—and after being battered and tormented by the violence, the storm subsided and we made it through.

By this point, Bobbi was just shattered. We got blown all the way back to Little Abaco in the Bahamas. I decided to get to the island through a little passage, so I didn't have to go through the main island (I did this to avoid being detected). When I tried to slither through, I had maybe two feet on either side of the cut. All the locals were watching, as I was trying to gauge the tide coming out and the waves going in. Nobody brings this size boat through this cut, I thought. And I learned why. I'd go forward about three feet and then go back about two, and I limped in there trying to make it through the tight space and the unfriendly tides.

All these locals watching were thinking that I was going to crash and then they'd be able to scavenge the boat when I did.

Eventually, I made it through, and all the people watching let out a huge cheer. I dropped into the back side of a small island with no inhabitants and slept all night long. We were fucking exhausted.

When we got up, we went through a main pass to Little Abaco, so I was planning on going through a cut that was really wide. But the tide carried me out of the channel and one of my pontoons got caught on a rock ledge. So I got hung up, I checked the tide charts and knew I'd be able to get out in about an hour or two. The locals who were all sailing by and laughing and thinking that I didn't know what I was doing. Little did they know all I had been through.

When I got to land, I ate so much fucking conch, and then I got some ice cream from a supply boat. I traded them a generator for a 3-gallon tub of chocolate ice cream, and I sat there and ate as much as I could before I had to toss it since we didn't have a freezer. I can't tell you how much of it I dusted, but I can tell you a man has never enjoyed a tub of chocolate ice cream as much as I did that day.

In Little Abaco, we were eating in a little place there when one of the locals said—loud enough for me to hear—that the police were coming the next morning to do a sweep. They were kindly tipping us off that it was time to leave. From there, I sent Bobbi home, and Sevi and I left on the boat early the next morning.

We made it to Daytona Beach, and our team sent out a commercial fishing boat to make contact with us. When they pulled up, they shouted at me, using the nickname of one of the weasel guards at Eglin, "Barney Fife is looking for you. Barney Fife is looking for you."

I knew it was Tommy when he used that joke about the guard—he was referring to the name of a fictional sheriff that he not-so-affectionately used for the prison guards we knew. Tommy was the guy I met in prison who started this whole thing. I don't think that son of a bitch did a hard thing in his life, so when he got there, I threw a bale at him and said, "Here, it's about time you did some honest work."

We quickly offloaded about 4,500 pounds, because that's all they could handle in the boat they brought. Well, I still had 6,500 pounds left to unload, so they had to come out the next night. I waited 24 hours, offloaded another 4,500 pounds, so I still had one ton of pot left.

The weather was starting to kick back up again, and they wanted me to turn around, go back into the Atlantic and kill a couple of days until they could organize another boat to get the rest. While they were deciding what to do, I motored along the coast of Florida about a half-mile off-shore headed south with 2,000 pounds of pot on it.

This vessel looked like fuck. Beat up from the storm, smoke blowing out of it (not from me smoking, just in case you were wondering), just about this close from looking like it was in distress. Well, as luck would have it, a routine Coast Guard patrol spotted me.

At that point, I couldn't alter my course. If I changed anything I was doing, that was going to give them reason to check me out.

"John, I'm not going out there. I'm not going through another fucking storm," I said, referring to the fact that I wasn't going back into the Atlantic Ocean. "I'm going to be a half-mile to a mile off-shore heading south down to Hillsborough Inlet. If you want to send a boat to catch up with me, you go right ahead. But I'm not changing my course."

That night at about 1 in the morning, I was off Palm Beach, and a huge Coast Guard cutter pulled right up on me.

Fuck. This is jail time.

I just knew there was no way of getting out of this. We had a literal ton of pot on board, and if the Coast Guard came on board, we were toast.

I told Sevi to get ready to throw the guns overboard. If we were going to get arrested, I said that I'll do the time for the pot, but I wasn't going to take a gun charge.

The Coast Guard shadowed me—remember, they didn't have top-notch technology back in the late 1970s—for about 45 minutes a couple hundred feet from me. No radio contact, no nothing. They hovered a couple hundred feet from me and did nothing. Then they left.

I called Bobbi at 3 in the morning.

"You need to hop in a little boat and head to Hillsborough Inlet, and I'll meet you the sea buoy at 5 o'clock."

"Well why do you need me to do that?" he asked.

"I need you to check for the marine patrol and take these girls off the boat," I said. He had no idea I was talking about the guns, but he did meet me there.

"You can take these guns, or I'll throw them in the water," I said, "but I'm just not going to go under that bridge with these guns on the boat."

He saw that the coast was clear, and we headed into Hillsborough Inlet and went right back to the dock where we left from. We still had that ton of pot on the boat, but the mission was accomplished.

We made it through the storm, the close call with the Coast Guard, the milk bottle dropping to the bottom of the ocean, the massive detour we had to take, the sail ripping apart, all of it. It was a trip of a fucking lifetime—and I probably aged a fraction of a lifetime during those few months.

We did it. We goddamn did it. We smuggled a boat load of weed.

When we tied up the boat to the dock, I got on my hands and knees. I kissed the dock, and then I looked at the heavens and said, "Fuck you, Richard Nixon."

CHAPTER 14

PARTY TIME

Damn. We did it.

When we arrived at the dock of a friend's house (she was a friend of Sevi's mother), we had to get inside to use the phone to tell them we had the rest of the weed. But it was locked, so we had to break a window to get inside. Right back from a fucking smuggle and we had to do a B&E—breaking and entering—to finish the job.

"We're here. You need to get this shit off the boat."

At Sebastian Inlet, near Stuart, Florida, we had a stash house, because that's where we had planned to end up. That was the plan: Roll up, stash the house. But because it took so much time at sea, the passage closed at Sebastian Inlet.

When we made contact, my contacts took me to the stash house and told me to get some sleep. There was a girl at the house. I slept real hard.

When I woke up, guys came in and started throwing piles of money at me. Here, here, here, here. Cash, cash, cash, cash. They were already selling the 9,000 pounds that they had picked up.

That's when they solidified my deal: I could have cash or a percentage of the load, meaning I could keep and sell a portion of the pot. The original load of 9,000 pounds turned out to be 11,000 pounds, so I did a quick calculation to tell me that I could make a lot more money by taking a percentage of the load and selling it.

"I'll take a percentage of the load," I told them, and got 1,100 pounds, which I could turn into a big party.

I called my ground crew at St. Pete Beach—mainly a guy named Tony, who came from a Hollywood family. Tony was key to my early success. He was a wiry guy who loved fucking fat women. "Best pussy there is," he'd say.

"Tony," I told him, "I got a thousand pounds of pot over here. You need to get the vehicles and get over here and sell it for me."

And they did. I didn't have to do a thing. Well, if you consider all the work I did to bring the pot back, then I guess you can say I more than earned my money. I just hung out and took the money when he sold it.

There's not another business in the world like it. What an honorable profession among people who are "criminals." All on a handshake. I trust them with my pot, they sell it, keep their share, and give me mine. I give up a thousand pounds of pot and got nothing for it up front—just a handshake and their word that I'd get my piece when it was sold. And I got it all back.

The next day after getting up at the house, the old guy on the offload boat drove me into Stuart. I was a mess. I needed a new wardrobe, so I bought a bunch of new clothes.

Then the party started. And never seemed to end.

To celebrate the successful smuggle, the principal players got a table at the fanciest and most exclusive place in West Palm Beach. A French restaurant, of course. There were probably 20 of us—me, my crew, the principals, the Colombians, hookers.

We were drinking Dom, eating fancy dinners, snorting cocaine, and gave the maître d' (who was a friend of the family) an ounce of cocaine and a thousand dollars to take good care of us that night. A victory dinner like no others.

I was the captain, and most of these guys had never met the man who drove the boat. They treated me like God, and I felt like a huge celebrity because what I did and who I was. The captain of the god-damn smuggle boat.

At one point, one of the guys deep in the marijuana industry in south Florida turned to me and said, "Don't ever get out of this business. You're good for this business."

That was a pretty powerful thing to say. I haven't forgotten that. (And it's crazy that I really haven't quit the business—all these years later.)

After that dinner, Tommy, John, and I started to party in Pompano Beach and Fort Lauderdale.

To do so properly, I bought a bunch of cocaine.

These two guys had always busted my ass, calling me a St. Pete Beach boy, and saying I couldn't keep up. Tommy and John were big players at the beach and bars, chasing women and having a good time. Big partiers. Remember that when I first met Tommy at Eglin, I told him he couldn't keep up with me running around the prison. Now, they wanted to turn it around and challenge me. They said, "Here, you can't keep up down here with us. This is our town."

So we started this contest to see who could party hard and long with all this cocaine.

John tapped out after three days. He just couldn't hang. Tommy? The two of us went head-to-head for 17 fucking days. Hardly any sleep, lots of liquor, lots of sex, lots of cocaine, and lots of Haagen Dasz ice cream. I don't think we ate real food for two weeks—just that fucking ice cream. Parties at one of our apartments, hanging out in the bars, girls hanging off our arms.

It went by in a flash. I had an obligation to celebrate after all. I had been working a lot of years in my life to get to this point, and I felt like I needed to party in the way I deserved—and the way I could now afford. We'd go to the bars with two or three girls each and have kamikazes for breakfast—after spending all night drinking and fucking. The girls were just into sexual athleticism back then—party girls, they were. Once, Tommy saw a girl walking the street with groceries and he said, "You want to do some cocaine?" She dropped her groceries and said, "Sure!" They were just into it back then. Women were just accessories. I hate to say it that way now, but it was just the era. They didn't know anything about the business and we didn't want them to. They hung out, partied, had a good time, and fucked us like crazy.

With cocaine, you'd never get drunk. You'd just keep going—and do a bump if you got tired.

At one point, I do remember sleeping about two or three hours and waking up with a huge rock of cocaine. We had a big, long kitchen counter in our party house. I started chopping the coke up and laying out three- or four-foot lines on the counter. Just a massive amount of cocaine. I did one line for me, and one for Tommy. I didn't wait for Tommy to wake up, so I did mine—and it knocked me against the fucking wall. When Tommy woke up, I said, "Well, you're behind."

Finally, at the end of it all, Tommy had to tap out.

"See, you can't keep up with me," I jabbed.

The next day, Tommy's son—who was just old enough to drive—took me to Tampa, because I still needed to meet with my parole officer. I stretched out and slept in the back of that Cadillac the whole way there and then got a hotel room at the Tampa airport so I could sleep some more.

Now, this winter was a brutal one, even for Florida. It was cold and pretty miserable. But when I walked into that parole office, I was dripping with sun—my hair was blonde and my skin was golden brown. I was at fucking sea for a couple of months and on top of the world. I had just made a shit ton of money.

When I walked into the office—which was made up of mostly women—it felt like a slow-motion reel of a movie star walking by. The whole room just looked up and fucking lit up. I'm bouncing, ecstatic, looking great. I checked in and had no problem with my federal parole officer (I think she wanted to get with me, actually, so that may have helped). All was good.

At the time I was living in Tarpon Springs, but I ended up buying a little house with a dock in Madeira Beach, which wasn't too far. The house was for sale, but it had a contract on it. The agent told me that if the contract fell through, I had a chance, but I had to put down a good down payment.

"How's 20 grand?"

She said that was fine.

Because I had changed districts when I moved, I had to get a new parole officer, who spent quite a bit of time trying to figure out who

I was and what the fuck I was doing. He was going up in the church tower with local police monitoring people and cars going in and out of my house. He was dedicated to the fact that I was up to no good, and he was trying to piece this puzzle in his brain. I had an answering service, so I knew when someone was calling and could listen in. This parole officer called asking if they kept receipts for my phone service. Then the service asked me if I heard that. I said, yeah, I did and I'll be right down to pick up the receipts myself so the parole officer couldn't get his hands on them.

I got the receipts, drove across the Skyway Bridge, and threw them all in Tampa Bay. So I called the federal officer and fucked with him. This was all part of the game: Feds vs. Heads.

After I bought the house in Madeira, I grabbed a girl—stole someone's girlfriend actually—and took off to party in California. I had a reputation for taking whichever chick I wanted.

In California, I just spent so much cash—buying furniture for my mom, buying clothes, drinking thousand-dollar bottles of wine, paying for a month's worth of hotel rooms with cash up front. In one of the hotels, there were two levels of shopping. In a nice jewelry shop, I bought a key chain made of pure gold—that was the one souvenir I wanted. In the wine shop, I bought the three best bottles of Bordeaux for every year from 1946 (the year I was born) to 1978.

This is what I was after. The good life. The high life. Living large with lots of cash, lots of partying, lots of sex, lots of drugs.

I was still on federal parole when I finished the smuggle, and I got off parole at the end of the year.

"What do you want to do now that you're off parole?" my partners would say to me.

I had an easy answer: I wanted to hit the road. I had been restrained too long.

So I became the Colombia connection: Running the cover business like buying and selling cars and shipping them to Colombia. Damn, there was so much corruption there. I had met the Colombian contacts at our big celebration party—must have been like 10 of them there. The principals, the ground crew, a bunch of them.

It was all a cover so we could smuggle drugs out of the country.

We'd fly down there (it was something like a two-hour flight), land at a clandestine air strip, take the weed and go. You could fit something like 4,000 pounds on the bigger planes, because we'd rip out the extra seats of a six-passenger plane and just go with two people.

The way it worked in Colombia at the time was that everybody was in on the deal—the cops, the military, all of them. You'd give them cash to look the other way when you were doing your work, and you had a small window to get it done. If you didn't finish in that window, then all bets were off—they could bust you. And they'd keep their money.

We didn't worry much about what happened in Colombia. The hard part was getting it back into the U.S.

But I lost my way, lost control of the business, and I didn't pay as much attention as I should have.

One plane that I had arranged crashed coming out of Colombia and the two pilots died. And one time, we had a plane coming into Riohacha, a city in northern Colombia. On that trip, coming out of the mountain, we got stopped by a military group. They hauled us into a military base. But one of our contacts was related to one of the old military commandants, and that helped us get off. We got out of the country after that, because one of the planes had a problem.

Another time, we went up into the mountains. To get there, we had to get in a boat and haul it up-river to a village that you could only access my boat. My role: Pick out the bales for a load. I was well-loved and well-established, and they respected me.

When we got to the village, they showed me several bales from villagers. Then we got to a man's house, sat in his courtyard, and were enjoying a beer when a gate opened.

There was a whole fucking parade of burros with bales of pot on their back. Every farmer was there for me to inspect their bales and see if I wanted to buy their pot. There must have been 30 of them. We spent all afternoon looking at pot. I didn't see anything I liked, so I turned them down.

I kept pointing at my moustache—a blondish-red shade—and telling them that's the color of weed I wanted. I wanted Santa Marta Gold Bud or Cali Red Bud, and they didn't have it. So that trip yielded nothing.

The only way you can do anything in Colombia is to do it with their families, and during my time, I worked with three of the five main drug families.

I never was able to get anything home. I had a great contact who was a relative of politicians, but it never panned out.

I wouldn't trade that experience for the world though. My passport has 13 stamps for Barranquilla, Colombia, on it. What a beautiful sea town, not too far from Santa Marta, another beautiful part of the country. Just gorgeous. During one stretch, I stayed there for six months straight. I felt like I was part of their family. Hell, some even tried to make that sentiment official. All the Colombian girls were like, "Marry me. Take me to Miami." They all wanted to just get to Miami. I could have gotten married like 10 times a day. At one point, my contact even wanted to give me a 1,000-acre ranch and build an airstrip on it to be the main point to go in-and-out of the country and smuggle weed. Fuck, I'm not living in fucking Colombia, but that's how close I got to the family. I had their trust.

I had a lot of great times (I remember fucking a girl so loud in this crappy hotel that everyone the next morning looked at us when we came into the lobby—"oh, that's them," they were saying). And I had some interesting ones (like the time the military raided a bar and threw us up against a wall, but they were just looking for guns, not drugs). Now, I was always careful and always went out in public with a Colombian, because they were getting $50,000 a head for a kidnapped American. I'd stay there for a week or so at a time, except the time I stayed for six months. And I don't regret any of it. Was I pissed I never had a successful air smuggle? Yeah, for sure. But I don't blame anyone but myself for not running it as tightly as I should have.

This all lasted about three years, and I just couldn't do it anymore. So that's when I went back to fishing.

When I was back in Florida, that real estate agent called me and said the contract on the house in Madeira fell through. Two days later, I bought the house, and I put it in a blind trust, because I was smart enough not to put it in my name. I didn't want people looking into what I was doing with all this money.

One night, I was at a bar on St. Pete Beach. I had an ounce of coke in my jacket pocket. I took three girls back to my apartment and did the whole ounce of cocaine, and a young woman named Suzi was the only one left. I never was able to get rid of her after that.

Her family hated me. I was 30 or 31, and she was the girl impressed by a guy in a nice car. She was quiet, but she had our beautiful daughter and it's what kept us together for a few years. But she was a crazy-ass woman, and her family wouldn't see it. They thought I was doing evil things, because that's what Suzi did—she lied and she lied and she lied. (So much so that Suzi's family still hates me—one of Suzi's sisters came to town recently and said she had a bullet with my name on it because of the way I treated her sister. I'm thankful that my daughter, Emily, now sees what a crazy woman her mother was.)

One time, when Suzi was about five months pregnant with Emily, she went for an ultrasound, and she used her dad's pickup truck (I didn't have a car because I was fishing). When she pulled in, she clipped the corner of the condo with the truck and started sobbing.

"What's the matter?" I said.

"This may not be your baby," she said.

I fucking sent her back to her parents' house. They were not happy. Her dad came over to my house with his son and his son-in-law. When I got outside, I saw them—and her dad had a big billy club hiding behind his leg.

He swung on me.

I caught the fucking club and shoved it under his chin and put him on the fucking ground.

I'm 31 and a tough fucking fisherman. He's a drunk.

I'm fucking choking him to death and he's gasping.

"Ben," I said, "if you want to have a conversation, you come to my house and come in the door and act like a fucking gentleman, and we can have a conversation. But don't come over here and think you're going to beat my fucking ass."

Then I turned to his son and son-in-law.

"Now you two motherfuckers get back in your car before I work you over with this fucking club."

They ran away and got in the car.

I invited Ben in and told him he had the most fucked up kids I had ever seen in my life. So he turned around and—BOOOOM—caught me right in the nose.

I grabbed that poor man and just beat the dog piss out of him.

Eventually he left, went home, and was in bed for three days. Probably should have gone to hospital. Ever since then, that family has hated me with a passion because I took out their hero.

When I was in jail for cocaine charges years later, Ben visited me. I was stunned. He put his hand on the glass and told me I was family. He visited for a while then left. Nobody knew it at the time, but he had been diagnosed with brain cancer and only had a few months to live, so he was making amends. Nobody in his family ever knew that he made that visit to me—to tell me that he knew I was in the right.

Because of the success I had, I had a lot of people who wanted me to stay in the cocaine business. I got into it through a Cuban guy I met in Eglin.

And that's a whole different animal.

I got lost in the clouds and fumes of cocaine for three years. My drinking was out of control—my liquor bills at home were running $600 a week. Wine, whiskey, coke. Fuck. All of it.

There was huge demand for cocaine in the early 1980s. Everybody wanted to know about it, and everybody wanted a piece of it. But this changed everything. Pot was a peaceful drug. Cocaine was associated with guns and violence and serious shit.

It was also serious money, and that was the allure.

But I was so fucked up that I didn't pay attention to my main business and to what I was good at—smuggling.

I turned into the financier. I'd fund the smuggle and hire others to do it, but because I was partying so hard, I didn't have a good handle on everything. Deals fell through, shit didn't get done, and I spent a lot on deals that didn't work. You lose your money pretty fast when shit like that happens.

All this time, I think I've got a true friend in Tommy, so I handed everything to him and let him run with it.

Tommy, of course, is a con man. And a damn good one.

So I never made any more money, no more deals, and ended up partying and pissing away everything I made from the smuggle.

I sold the house to another guy named Randy, who was an attorney and became my attorney. Shit, I never should have sold it. I spent $70,000, and now that thing is worth over $1 million. But I gave Randy a good deal on it because I needed the cash. Randy later got busted for cocaine and lost his license. He ended up a successful businessman and author.

As for me, I wasn't doing real well.

I was out of money and out of cocaine.

And that's when I knew my alcohol problem was out of control.

The islanders call alcohol "the demon's rum." And I sure as hell know why.

CHAPTER 15

DRINKING MYSELF TO DEATH

I would drink until I'd pass out. I wasn't violent, and I wasn't mean. I just drank too much.

I'd drink up to a quart of whiskey a day.

When I ran out of money, I turned to fishing. Couldn't drink at sea, but you'd be drunk the entire time you were on shore. I turned out to be a good fisherman, so I could make a living and continue my drinking.

Grouper fishing in the Gulf. Loved it. And I was good at it.

Long-lining is like factory work at sea. (Long-lining is exactly what it says—you cast a long fishing line out with bait set at intervals to catch a massive amounts of fish as schools go by.) You catch a lot of fish that way, and it's non-stop work, like 20 hours a day. I was cap-taining some of the trips, or co-captaining them. Truth is, we were all working hard as a team anyway. I didn't drink out there. Can't do that, because you need your wits about you, though you do smoke a joint a day when you're on the water.

As a captain, I'd spend an hour first thing in the morning getting stuff ready, doing paperwork, then getting the crew up and ready to go. When you're long-lining, you sometimes have to haul in a load before you even eat breakfast.

To long line, we'd motor to the 80-, 90-, and 100-fathom breaks in the Gulf. At 40 fathoms, you have a hard break that goes from the Everglades to Panama City. Out there, you'd see fish you'd never seen before. We were catching ones called a Chocolate Grouper at 90 to 100 fathoms.

They were something like 90 or 100 pounds and would float up to the top. Fucking unbelievable. We'd put on a thousand pounds of fish before breakfast. That's fun as fuck. There's fishing and there's catching. That's catching.

After my mom had a heart attack, I moved out with her in Palm Springs for about a year and a half to help her. I was a bad, bad drunk. I passed out on her floor once. There was a local bar that had well drinks for 95 cents and I'd lay a $20 on the bar. One night, I got a DUI and as part of punishment, I had to go to an alcohol awareness class. Every night after that class, I'd go to a bar, get drunk and drive some more—just to prove that I could do it. I hated the mandated AA classes.

My daughter and her mother begged me to come back to Florida, so I did. And I went back to fishing. I was working hard, making good money. Our schedule was 12 days out and three days in, and you had to make 30 or more trips to make a decent living. It's damn hard work. Sometimes, it'd be a two-man operation, but most times, we were taking long-lining trips, which meant that it was five or six of us.

When I came back from California, I fished a little bit, but I started selling weed to the fleet as a way to make my money. All the captains would take a bag for their trips.

I was also drinking off and on during this time.

One day, my dad called me. He had run into my former mother-in-law in Indiana, and he asked if I would be interested in helping out with my son, Jason, who I hadn't seen since he was a year and a half old. I said yes, and next thing I know, I'm in Tampa airport picking up this 18-year-old, who had dropped out of school and was being a typical neighborhood punk committing small crimes. I found out some years later that a judge had told him he could either go to jail or move down with me.

Well, he thought it was pretty cool that his dad was selling pot. He didn't want his GED or to get a job, so I put him on a fishing boat, and that's what he did.

One night, I fell asleep in my car with the radio on and a big old joint in the ashtray. Weed in the back seat, Valium in the front seat. The cops came by and busted me for DUI, possession of pot. I ended up in jail and on house arrest for that quarter pound of weed.

I had this house arrest officer who was pure Gestapo. A harsh motherfucker.

I was working in the maintenance department for a motel, drinking all the time. I almost got my house arrest revoked—I just wanted to do my jail time for a few months rather than do this house arrest for two years. I knew I'd fuck it up, and I told my daughter's mother that I would.

"Well why would you fuck it up?" she said.

"Because I'm drinking too much," I said.

She went on to tell me that she thought my daughter would probably prefer that I quit drinking than go to jail.

That was the weekend in my life that I came to grips with my disease of alcoholism, and I knew I needed to quit.

Alcohol was my best friend.

I cried, and I cried, and I cried.

I didn't know a human being could cry as much as I did. But I sat in my apartment coming to grips with it all. All the stupid shit I did because of alcohol came flooding back. The misery. The heartbreak. The horrible shit you did to people who loved you just came back to me. Crying and crying and crying…

That's when I decided that was that.

All this bullshit I had delivered to people. All the pain I had inflicted on people. All the destruction I had done to people. It crashed down on me, and I knew I had to stop. Fuck, even when I stopped, I was still having dreams of being drunk. It was a hard thing to do—and a very hard thing to start.

After that conversation about Emily with her mother, I walked out of my apartment on a Sunday morning to go to my first real AA meeting out on Sunset Beach. It was literally a weekly meeting they had on the beach at 11 in the morning, where the whole community would migrate. My house arrest officer drove down the street and saw me. "Where are you going?"

"I'm going down here to an AA meeting," I said.

"Well," he said, "I think that's a good place for you. You are an alcoholic."

So I went up, sitting there, an emotional basket case. Some 50 people were there, and the week before I went was just a horrific week—where I really came face-to-face with my disease of alcoholism. It would take a long time to get over the damage I had done to my mind and body—not to mention my relationships—and I had a lot of repairing to do. I introduced myself to a few alcoholics, and there was so much support. All those people knew your pain, and they could see the pain. I ended up going to 90 meetings in 90 days with a neighbor. (It took me about six months before I started opening up to people.)

At that first meeting, my daughter and her mother walked up to join me. And I started sobbing and sobbing again.

CHAPTER 16

BUSTED FOR COKE

I took my white chip at the end of the meeting on March 17, 1989, and I haven't had a drink since.

I was done. I had completed my duty to alcohol.

Soon after, a guy who owed me money from a bad real-estate deal offered me some cocaine as a way to pay back his debt.

I told him I didn't want it. I didn't want it to be part of my life. I was done.

He kept pushing me, kept bugging me.

Fine. I made a call and made a sale. I sold it and made a quick five grand.

Well, the guy I sold it to had a girlfriend who was all freaked out about it, so he asked me if I could store it for him while he tried to sell it. I put some back in my house, and fuck, I started playing with it. One of my fishing buddies who my son fished with had a hot little Italian friend named Michelle, and I was trying to get with her (and her friend in a three-way if you must know). She wanted to take some cocaine to sell it, and she did.

I had been getting high and was hiding two kilos in the house. I had called a couple hookers from an escort service. That night, Michelle called me and said she wanted to bring me the money for the cocaine sales. I told her not to come (I had hookers coming!).

So we were waiting for the hookers to come, and a car pulled in. A guy got out of the car. And I'm thinking he's one of the guys who was doing security for the hookers, making sure it was the right place for the girls.

I was waiting on the porch and the guy—and all these hooded ninja motherfuckers—start coming out of the shadows.

The fucking drug task force.

I tried to slam the door, and they slammed me on the ground. My buddy went to get out of there, and they slammed him on the ground.

I knew that none of the coke was in plain view, so I told them they needed to get a warrant—the Plain View Principles (you can go in but you can't open anything). And they couldn't reach my probation officer, which would have given them the legal right to just go in and search. So they were fucked. No warrant. No reason to go in.

They went into my house and went straight to the cocaine.

Little Michelle had told them where it was.

She had been busted for the ounce of coke, so she was working with Clearwater Police to stay out of jail.

The cops took it all and then took us to jail. They also caught my buddy with a rock of cocaine. The fucker had stolen it from me and put it in a sweater and hid it in his motorcycle helmet. So I was like, fuck him, that's his cocaine. (Just like that little fucker from Iceland who bought my 8-page porn book when I was kid—it's his now, not mine!)

In the station, I saw Michelle and asked her if she was ok, and I told the cops almost everything. I didn't fuck anybody else (Michelle ended up with six months of probation), but they took me to a maximum-security jail and charged me with possession with intent to distribute cocaine, and then they raised my bail to a quarter million bucks. They were threatening 27 years of jail because they wanted me to give up my contacts. Well, I wouldn't give them up, but I did tell them that there was more cocaine.

"I've got more at a friend's house. I tell you where it is, but you must promise me that you won't arrest them. If you make that promise, I'll take you there."

Well fuck, they put me in a squad car, went up to the house, then went in to take all the cocaine, but didn't arrest anybody in.

That showed me something pretty powerful: The real interest of the cops isn't fucking with people but getting this stuff off the streets. As long as you've got good cops like that, you've got good cops.

But I'm still fucked. I'm in max security for 26 months. Lights on all day. Waiting. Battling over a bad search. While I was there, I got into a drug program for three months, like an AA meeting, listening to kids telling horror stories about crack cocaine. Fucking sad and depressing.

While I was there, I worked as the jail librarian, a decent job. Inmates would put in requests, and I'd deliver their reading orders. The guards would get week-old magazines and throw in porn in the big tubs. You're not supposed to have that stuff in jail, but they wanted to read fucking porn while they were on duty. They'd give me coffee and pie and all kinds of shit in exchange for the porn.

They also started a program called Changing Criminal Thoughts, with the theory that rehab is not possible. You got to change the way people think before you change behavior. I worked on that program—in there with murderers and rapists and really bad people. You tend to think that if you're in there for drugs, then you're not a real criminal. Well, fuck, you're eating the same food and wearing the same clothes, so you're a fucking criminal. For 16 months, I was in that program and stayed active in AA. A couple nights before Christmas in 1992, they released me. Home for the holidays.

They set the trial date for September of the next year. Now out of jail just waiting for the trial date, I had to get a job doing some warehouse work. I tried to get back on my feet. When I was in jail, a counselor said that I automatically qualified for the Pell Grant because I hadn't had income in two years.

Soon after, I read in the paper that the two highest demanding jobs in the future would involve either psychology or physical therapy.

From my time in AA, I learned a lot. AA was a place that didn't like religion too much; hell, most of the people I met in AA were recovering Catholics. Organized religion fucked up people so bad—"because I said so" as a way of thinking is not good enough. The Sermon on the Mount, which I read in my early days in AA, was a powerful book for me. The first time I read it, I cried big tears, because it explained all the shit I was supposed to learn about Jesus's teachings—stuff I should have learned as a kid but nobody ever taught. It changed my way of thinking, because it was about how to live righteously. We actually started a small group of people who would get together to talk about the message and the book. That book was the relief valve I needed.

I also learned that the mind is not a place where I wanted to live in terms of my career, so studying psychology was out.

The mind is a deep, dark, dirty place to play. I don't want to be in people's heads. Physical therapy—bones, muscles, tissues, all that shit—that sounded like a much better path. I hadn't been in college in 23 years. All the drugs, all the booze, all the shit. Hell, I didn't even know if my brain still worked.

But I went over to St. Pete College and introduced myself.

"Hi, I'm Gary Kinsey. I've been locked up for two years, and I want to go back to college. Can I?"

"Yeah, you can," they said.

"Ok, let's go."

CHAPTER 17

GETTING HIGH—ON EDUCATION

I signed up for a two-year program to be a physical therapy assistant, not knowing how—or if—my brain was going to work. I was 47 years old, more than twice the age of most students and essentially a peer of my professors.

I took four or five classes a semester, studied all the time, and went to AA meetings. I didn't have a car at first (I had lost my license for five years), so I had to ride my bike to the bus stop, take a bus, then go back.

That was my life. I picked up all my science and math and all the classes to get me caught up before the PT program. In fact, I took math every semester because I knew I needed the discipline to work on math. My first semester, I took baby algebra, because everybody had to take it. About five weeks into that class was when my brain started functioning again in math. Before that, it was hard to focus living on the beach, but I had a humanities teacher who told us a story about a guest speaker who said there were two keys to being successful in college: go to class every day and do your homework.

I said to myself, "I can do that." And I did. Never missed a class, never missed my homework, and I realized I needed to be doing my math homework to keep me sharp, disciplined, and on track. There, I met some teachers who became my friends—one of them named Judy, who I hung out with, along with another math teacher. We went to the beach, went out to eat, just hung out. Judy would stay a dear friend and, in many ways, changed the course of my life a few years down the road.

After the first year, I had a 4.0 and joined an honor society (not too shabby for a pot smuggler!), where I made a nice group of friends. That's when I started to pick up more and more hard classes. All the time, I was clean—clean from booze and drugs. My brain was clear, and I felt great. (This proved to me that we tell a whole bunch of lies to ourselves saying weed destroys brain cells. Once I stopped, my brain was as sharp and high-functioning as it ever was—probably even more so. After 25 years of hard drinking and drugging, I went back to college and excelled in my academics. I hadn't killed brain cells. I just needed to get them fired up again.) I stayed off of weed for a total of six years, and I haven't had a drink since that day I stopped in 1989.

I was so excited to be a student again. My brain had focused on the cannabis business for decades, and I was happy to have my brain firing again. It was a whole new experience for me, and I just embraced it. The teachers loved me, probably just because I was their age—and probably because I was interested in school, unlike a lot of the students in junior college who were just there to be there. I wanted to do sports physical therapy because it seemed like a fun path to pursue.

One of my classmates got me a job in a physical therapy clinic in Largo, Florida, as an aide, so I held a part-time job while going to school. At the clinic, there were two Dutch-trained therapists along with two American-trained ones.

In my second year in college, the honor society teamed up with USA Today for something called the Florida All-Star Academic Team, a contest where you had to write essays and do all kinds of other stuff. At one point, those who did really well were asked to visit Tallahassee (the state capitol), and all of the honorees were called to the state legislature for our names to be read into the record as outstanding scholars. Afterwards, there was a big spread at the governor's mansion to honor us. "These are the kids I want in my college," said Betty Castor, president of the University of South Florida at the time, and she offered a group of students full-ride scholarships at USF. I didn't qualify, but I asked her about USF's physical therapy program. Unfortunately, USF didn't have PT programs so I couldn't go. I would have gone there if they did.

I graduated St. Pete College after three years and was accepted into an international physical therapy program in Holland at the University of Amsterdam Polytechnical Institute called Hogeschool von Amsterdam.

In college, I had heard rumors that there was a recruiter trying to get American students to go to Holland to study physical therapy. The demand in the U.S. was so high—so many students wanted to go to PT school, but most programs were only letting in a few dozen students a year, so they couldn't keep up with the demand. In

Holland, they had overdeveloped their PT education, but they didn't have many jobs, so few people were signing up for the education. The recruiter had an idea: Get American students who wanted to pursue physical therapy into the programs in Holland, where they needed students. Put American students in Holland's empty seats. Made perfect sense. So they collaborated to start a program called American Stream Physical Therapy, which lasted five years.

After I graduated from St. Pete College, I had to sell all my belongings to get ready to go to Amsterdam—43 of us from all over the United States. We met at Tampa International Airport to fly over together and start our two-year program.

There, we lived in apartments in a little village called Reigerbos outside of Amsterdam, about a mile from the college and the teaching hospital. It was a beautiful, quaint little village. I just loved it. And I loved Amsterdam and everything around it.

We'd usually walk or ride our bikes everywhere. I swear to God, before we even got unpacked, we had Jehovah's Witnesses ringing our doorbell. "Fuck, we can't get away from these people anywhere!" I told my three roommates.

We had to bring cash with us to cover our living expenses (literally, like cash in a bag). Our tuition was paid for us, but the deal was that we had to work for the group when we returned from the program at $38,000 a year to pay off that tuition loan. I got $20,000 as an early inheritance from my grandmother to bring to Holland to cover my expenses. She loved me, and she was so happy I had quit booze and drugs and was in recovery.

In school, I was 20 or so years older than my classmates. They were going to the clubs in Amsterdam—a 20-minute train ride—on the weekends and doing ecstasy and all that shit. I didn't have any desire to do it—even in a country where weed was legal. I wasn't there to smoke; I was there to study.

For the first six months, I was very focused on my courses and learning all I could about physical therapy. I really wanted to get everything straight. I did explore a little bit, walking along tram lines and biking on the trails (99 percent of Dutch people ride bikes, no doubt). Just a beautiful city and beautiful country. I loved the people. I stopped to talk to people all the time. My classmates would all hang together, but I was a lone wolf, doing my own thing. It was a palpable feeling of love I had for Amsterdam and the people of Holland.

In the program, we were covering all kinds of subjects—the physiology stuff you'd expect in a PT program. But we also took a lot of psychology classes too. Crazy, right? I had no desire to play in the brain at all, because I know how fucked up our brains are. But in this program, they treated the body holistically. Makes a lot of fucking sense when you think about it. When you're injured or disabled or have some other kind of physical limitation, your mind takes a big hit. Therapy and healing are as emotional as it is physical.

We'd do this at the clinic where I worked too. When someone would come in, we didn't just ask about what happened injury-wise, but we'd ask them what they were thinking and feeling. It's complete and holistic, which is not the approach we take in the United States. Here, it's injury-fix-injury-fix. But in Holland, we'd do all kinds of pain-relief courses and learn techniques that aren't allowed in the U.S. My theory: Those techniques and skills we were learning stopped pain after one or two treatments, and the pharmaceutical companies certainly wouldn't want that. That's a fucking travesty.

We also learned manual skills—joint and spinal mobilization—and massage techniques. Hell, we took massage courses every semester for two years. It was so different than anything students learned in the U.S. (I later worked with a Mayo-trained therapist, and he had no fucking idea how to even do a massage to help with healing.)

Six months into the program, I had my bearings. I was still exploring and loving all the sights and people of Amsterdam.

One day, on one of my journeys, I saw a sign at a coffee shop.

"Nepalese Hash Balls"

We had our Christmas party coming up and my Secret Santa was the youngest kid in class—a guy named Jeremy from Michigan. One time, I had asked him if he ever had any good hash. He said he didn't know—didn't know what the difference between good hash and funk hash was. So for his Secret Santa present, I got him a chunk of Nepalese Hash Balls. That was my first time in a coffee shop in Amsterdam since I was there. I had had no designs on smoking, but I wanted to get Jeremy some good stuff, and I figured I'd buy a couple grams for the party for my classmates.

Back at my apartment, I sat at my desk and started rolling the joints for my classmates.

Immediately, it was in my mouth and I sparked a joint.

Six years completely clean and sober.

And now, I'm smoking some damn fine weed.

That shit started popping and cracking and firing up my brain. I could feel it. I could hear the electric circuitry going on my brain. Immediately, I started thinking about what they teach you at AA: With addiction, it's like tapes playing over and over in your brain, and the longer you're sober, the more that the electric circuit goes away. So I immediately had the scary thought: Is smoking this joint going to lead me to drink again. Thank God, it never did.

My roommates came home, and they started saying, "Oh my God, Gary's smoking pot. Oh no, what are we going to do?" They were all kinda freaked out about it at first. I ended up bringing it to the party, and everybody got stoned, and I never looked back.

Pot was back in my life. Forever.

CHAPTER 18

PAIN PRINCIPLES

In school in Amsterdam, I mostly smoked on the weekends. No point in smoking before class. There was too much shit to learn, to know, to be sharp about.

There, we had to do practical exams periodically throughout our course work. They'd give us a body part, and we had to study everything we knew about that body part for 24 hours. One time, they gave me the ankle. So we were studying and studying and studying every goddamn thing about the ankle. Then we'd go to some small clinic in Holland where they'd give us our practical examination.

On my second practical exam, I knew every damn thing about the ankle. I was ready. But I had an hour bus ride to get to the clinic, so I figured I'd smoke a joint before I left—plenty of time for me to re-focus before being tested.

When I got there, it was a fucking amphitheater. All the teachers and therapists were up high watching down in the room.

My exam: A girl whose ankle was so fucked up that I was flabbergasted. What the fuck. I'm looking at it and not knowing what to do. It's such a mangled mess I don't know how to fix it.

"You don't know what you're doing, do you?" the clinician said to me.

I replied, "I don't have a clue. I've never seen anything like this in my life."

I failed that practical exam, and I learned a lesson: When you need to think critically, don't smoke pot.

In school, I needed to have my brain cleaned out and clear so I could just go and go and go, and not trail off in all different trains of thought the way it is when you smoke.

After my first year, I took an internship at a clinic in Holland—all focused on physio therapy. They only used two modalities to treat patients, and they treated top athletes: Ice and massage. I remembered we used this technique called cross-fiber friction massage, grabbing the muscle to massage it. It was a violent healing technique, but it worked to break up that tissue so it could heal properly and not be all fucked up when it did. Then we'd ice the injury with tons of ice on a heavy towel on the injury. They had to bear it for 20 minutes—most painful thing in the world for the first few minutes. But both techniques were so incredibly effective. Unbelievable. I learned so much about the body and injuries, and I saw such things in my coursework like e-stimulation and super intensive electrotherapy, which weren't allowed in the United States. We use big-pharma profit pills to supposedly heal here in the U.S.

In one of my journeys off campus, I discovered a nice little pot shop called Kadinsky's. Every eighth day, they had a sale—20 percent off their whole menu: dozens of kinds of weed, coffees, juices. That was my refuge. Nobody in my class knew about it for a while. It was my time to smoke, meet people, talk, enjoy Amsterdam.

During my time, I did have a few love interests. Hell, the Dutch women with those long legs? I fell in love a million times a day. In my first neuro lab, the professor had an aide—a 6-foot-2 red-headed Dutch girl. Wow. Fell in love immediately with her. She made me dinner (that's what they do there for first dates). I asked her if she had a boyfriend.

"Yes," she said.

"No," she then said.

"I don't know," she then said.

And I'm thinking what the fuck. Story was that she had a boyfriend from New Zealand who didn't like Amsterdam, and she didn't like New Zealand, so they were living in different places.

We ended up becoming friends, and she told me about the best internship in Holland—a place where no American had ever worked. I lobbied hard to get there and did get the internship. There, I worked a lot with stroke patients and pediatric patients. What a tough job working with kids with birth defects. I learned a lot about pain there too, like fibromyalgia, where I saw that was a real thing—and people really deal with a lot of shit when they're in pain.

At the school, there was an employee named Sacha, also a long-legged Dutch girl. I flirted with her a bit.

One Friday night, I asked her, "Are you going out to drink a beer?

"I can't tonight," she said, "but I can sometime."

Damn, I think I just got a date with Sacha. We ended up having a relationship and had lots of fun. We'd go to the parks, and we'd go to the beach. One time, she took me to a clothing-optional health spa.

That was nice. I moved in with her during my last stretch of school, and we had a nice little relationship for a while.

When I graduated from PT school in 1998, we had our ceremony at Madeira Beach, where our program started.

I had done 26 months in school—just like the 26 months I had just done in prison before that. And I look back at that time, thankful for the fact that that's what I needed to get sober.

My next mission: Get my state license. I was back in Florida, and I was ecstatic. I had done five years of intense education, I had learned so much, I had written a thesis about "bookbag shoulder," I had seen and treated so many patients, I had learned about the human body, and I had mastered techniques that would be so helpful for people trying to heal. I wanted to work in a rehab clinic, for sure. I couldn't handle a hospital job—too much red tape and bureaucracy.

And I liked the idea of sports rehab and stroke rehab.

Before I had even started college, I called the state and told them about my history. I asked, "Can I become a physical therapist?"

They said I could because therapists don't handle drugs, so it's not a problem—I would just need to have my civil rights restored. I figured that wasn't a big deal. I had done my time.

When I graduated in November 1998, I got turned down for licensure, because I couldn't get my voting rights back due to Florida laws.

I fought and fought and fought, all the time working for an organization that helped low-income, disabled people survive. My organization had some state pull, so they were able to fast-track me to see the state clemency board, headed by Governor Jeb Bush and other high-profile Florida politicians.

During my presentation—my plea to get my civil rights restored and voting rights back so I could then get my license to practice physical therapy—I brought my daughter so they could see I was doing honest work and was responsible. I was a different man than the one who had been busted, who had smuggled 11,000 pounds of pot, who lived the cocaine life years earlier.

I had five minutes to present my case.

"I'll take this under consideration," the governor said. "I'll get back to you in a couple of weeks."

I'm thinking, well, he didn't say no.

Two weeks later, I got a call from the clemency board.

"The governor has denied your request."

No reason given. No explanation. No fucking nothing. You're playing with people's lives and you won't fucking tell them why you're doing it?

I realized I wasn't going to be able to practice physical therapy in Florida—my home. I could have practiced it in 43 other states, but not Florida. I wanted to be here.

Fuck it. I knew there was nothing I could do to win. I decided I would go back to Holland. After all, I had an international license. I could practice there.

CHAPTER 19

LIVING THROUGH LOSS

I drove out to California in November 1999—a farewell tour to say goodbye to my mom, my grandmother, and my sister.

During that time, I talked to one of my favorite math teachers from St. Pete College—my old friend Judy. She was more than a teacher. She was my friend.

I told her I was going back to Holland, because I was never going to get my rights back in Florida.

"Gary, that's not you," she said. "You can't do that. You can't throw in the towel. You're a fighter. You can't leave and run away from this."

So I listened to her and I pursued the fight. Instead of going to Holland, I drove back from California to Florida, and I tried everything I could to get my rights restored so I could get my therapist license.

None of it worked.

I gave up, devastated, knowing that I'd never be a physical therapist in Florida.

It was frustrating as fuck.

But I had my degree, which is what really matters, and I started working those survival-type jobs. The main one was working for that center for independent living, helping poor and disabled people live independently in the community. I helped them with the bills, their logistics, running to the food bank. It was meaningful work—keeping people alive really.

At about this time in 2000, my nearest sister was diagnosed with Lou Gehrig's disease. Just a brutal and harsh disease. I spent a lot of time flying back and forth between Florida and Indiana to help care for her—and to help teach those caring for her what they could to help her, at least maintain some dignity. She had an incredible support system—a community of 16 women who gave back to her and did everything. These were former students, parents of students of hers, her sorority sisters, her teachers. They helped get her up, get her cleaned, take her out and about. They never let her quit living her life.

As my sister's disease progressed, she couldn't communicate besides just nodding her head. My dad didn't like me very much, but he loved his daughters, and it was so hard on him to see his daughter like this—her not being able to talk back. It was so devastating to him. Just horrible.

I would go up every other weekend to visit and to help as much as I could.

At one doctor's visit in August of 2001, we asked the team if there were any drugs in the pipeline that would help her fight the disease, they said no, and that was the day that my sister decided that the fight was over. The disease had won.

I came back on that Sunday night, hurt and sad about this latest development in my sister's health.

On Monday morning, I took a 20-mile bike ride before work. I had always loved to run and be fit. Being in PT school—where we all valued physical activity—I was in good shape. And at St. Pete College, I got a job in work study working in the exercise facility, so I got really good with exercise and equipment. I was in there hours a day. I was so fit. My thighs were like a running back's. "Man you got nice legs," people would say to me.

At the end of that Monday morning ride, I powered out the last mile. I was so hot, dripping and dripping.

I needed to go to work, so I took a cold shower and walked out dripping wet to stand under the ceiling fan. I went back and forth for about an hour, and I couldn't get cool.

Eventually, I got dressed and went to work—19 miles away in rush-hour traffic.

I felt some pressure building up in my chest, like an elephant sitting on it. So I thought, fuck, I might be having a heart attack. But I had an appointment and went to work. I told my friend John, who owned the clinic, that I could also help him with a patient he needed help with.

"Yeah, I can do that, John, but I gotta tell you, I might be having a heart attack," I told him.

He stuck his head in the door and told the patient, "Hey, holler if Gary falls over."

I finished the treatment, started my other appointment, and asked for aspirin. But nobody had any. The dentist who had the office next door was getting treatment and he said, "You're having a heart attack."

The ambulance picked me up quickly. We got to the ER in the hospital in Largo, and they pumped me full of morphine.

The doctor walked away, and then I heard him down the hallway yelling at the top of his voice.

"WHAT THE FUCK DO YOU MEAN THERE'S NO CARDIOLOGIST?"

He came back and said, "Gary, I'm going to do my best to keep you alive, but they don't have a cardiologist, and you need a stent right now."

They finally found one and he couldn't get a stent in—the right coronary artery was 100 percent blocked.

So they went in and did double-bypass surgery on me, and I didn't have any heart issues after that.

Just fucking crazy. My sister is dying of Lou Gehrig's, and I have a major heart attack. My dad is freaking out and asked if I wanted him to come, and I told him no.

"Just stay there and take care of Deeann," I told him.

As I recovered (my medical leave was a couple months), I still worked in my job and still made trips back and forth to Indiana. My boss needed me to come back to work as many hours as I could, so I didn't have to go on long-term disability.

My heart attack was in August 2001, and I returned to my office in time to see the Twin Towers fall. In June 2002, my sister died. At her eulogy, I spoke about the level of community support she had received. "This is what happens when you stay in a community and give back to it," I said. That's what my sister had done. She stayed in Indiana and had been a giving person to others—and so many people had given back to her in return.

In August 2002, my mother had a stroke. I rushed to California, and I made it to the hospital before she stroked out. I made it there to hug her and kiss her as she had her final stroke. I started yelling at the staff to come in, but nobody responded. It was too late.

She died in my arms.

In November 2002, my dad died of a massive heart attack on his kitchen floor after having sex with his crazy wife. That was a complete shock, because his doctor had told him that he was in perfect health at his annual physical three days earlier. But fucking, it turned out, would be what killed him.

All of this, as you might imagine, was heartbreaking. I was just rattled, and it took me a good three years before I got over the severe pain of experiencing that much loss in such a short amount of time.

I lost half my family in five months.

The human psyche. Fuck. I kept working, but I was fragile.

My job was to help people solve their problems, but it got to the point where my problems got so big that I couldn't help other people with theirs.

CHAPTER 20

TRANSITIONS

I had to leave the agency in 2003, because I just couldn't do it anymore. I was destitute. No income. And my mind wasn't in a place where I could work with people. All of this loss just crushed my soul. I didn't know how I was going to pay rent. I didn't know how I was going to eat. I didn't know how I was going to survive, so I went to the welfare office and asked for help. They approved me for food stamps and helped me get set up with the VA system because of my military background. That enabled me to get some disability checks. I wasn't working, and I wasn't in a mental place to do so. My kids were being assholes too. My son was lost in his drug addiction, and my daughter was acting out—disrespecting me, yelling and screaming in public at me, even accused me of choking her. She made that fucking lie up.

And my PTSD hit me hard after 2004.

That's the fucked-up thing about PTSD. Never had a lick of it my whole life, and then I got punched and punched and punched by the deaths in my family and being out of work, and it all hit me. PTSD from a life of hard living and hard times.

Fuck it. I left Pinellas County, where I had spent just about all of my Florida life, moving from beach town to beach town at various points.

I told my cats that we were out. We were going north.

I headed to the Itchetucknee—remember, this was the place in north Florida where we dried up our Missouri River funk weed. I found a place, started making friends, lived on disability, ate off the land—eating off fig trees and pecan trees, collecting blueberries. I met a woman who lived nearby, and she had massive blueberry bushes. (That's not a metaphor—I know I've been a crude guy, but c'mon.) Six giant ones. Every morning in blueberry season, I'd fill up five-gallon buckets with them. I made pies, I gave lots away, I ate some of them myself.

I lived there for four and a half years, trying to survive, figuring out how to deal with people again.

Slowly, I started to pull myself together.

Some of my friends from college were now in Gainesville, which was about an hour or so away.

One of my dearest friends said, "Gary, you gotta come back to work."

She hooked me up with a physical therapist named Bruce who had left his company because he didn't want to move up the corporate ladder. Bruce decided to set out on his own and start a mobile therapy company. He bought a trailer, set up shop there, and started a business providing mobile rehab services.

I interviewed with him and went to work with him, and I moved to Gainesville in 2009. I rented a cheap apartment, and then I found a great house for cheap. The owner loved long-term renters, and I jumped on it. And I've been there ever since. Together, Bruce and I built the company. I had skills people needed, though I wasn't technically licensed.

We did good work. We helped people.

After my grandmother died at 104 a few years later, I realized that I hadn't been paid properly. I was supposed to get a base salary and commission, but I wasn't being paid my commission. He was months behind, and I told him.

One Friday, when I got my check, I turned around and told the people in the office, "You call yourselves Christians, and you can't even pay a man for his work? Fuck you. I'm outta here."

I turned around and walked out the door.

On Monday, I went back in, and Bruce—who wasn't there on Friday—said, "Let's go get a cup of coffee."

So we went to McDonald's, had our coffee, and he was just stammering. I made it easy on him and just resigned. I helped him start and then build the business, even bought some of the equipment with my disability money and my wages from work. Bruce had put in hard work—he put in 90 hours a week, but he was trying to manage working with insurance companies, billings, and the complexities of working with someone like me, who couldn't go through insurance. He ended up having to pay me unemployment for a year because some of the billing and payment mistakes he made.

On unemployment in about 2012 or 2013, I got a notice about an entrepreneur training program for unemployed and under-employed college graduates. I decided to get involved with that. Sounded like a good opportunity, especially with my skill sets and life experiences.

The first presentation was stunning. This was all through the University of Florida—a powerhouse when it comes to innovation. The program was designed to help people like me learn small business skills. It was a 10-week program, and we formed teams of about seven or eight people headed by someone who was a successful entrepreneur.

This was especially great for people over 50 who had been hit by the economic downturn of 2008. We had all this brainpower, no work, and few possibilities to get hired. It was a brilliant idea for a program, I thought.

Working for Bruce and working largely with older people, I came to understand a thing or two about urinary tract infections—and how devastating they are to the older population and how expensive they are for hospitals. The problem is that they don't have the means to keep urinary bags and tubing in proper locations to ensure good drainage and not back up and cause infections. Well, you know what? The University of Florida had a patent on a low-tech device that would keep the tubing and the drainage bag in good orientation to have proper drainage from the bladder so people wouldn't get infections. I looked at the technology: It was simple, there's a huge demand for it, let me investigate it. The patent was written by a professor at UF, and I decided to take it and commercialize it. I got two people from my team from the program and some friends and asked if they wanted to be part of my team. They were all in.

We did the whole thing: business plan, created the device, all of it. It was fucking exciting.

Even though I was anti-corporation and anti-bureaucratic-bullshit for my whole life, there was something about this that really charged me up: I was using my brain, I was helping people, hell, all of my skills—as a missile engineer (the mechanics) and a drug dealer (the money, the negotiating)—were in play.

Let's see if we can pull this shit off.

We tried. I had some investors. I tried selling it to the local hospitals. I gave presentations to the nurses to show them how it would work. I manufactured 2,000 to 3,000 devices. This thing was going to work—to stop infections and save money.

But I was told that the device was too expensive. Bullshit. It was all health-care politics at play. After a series of conflicts with the powers that be at UF, I told them we were done—and that was the end of the device and the idea and my company. Nobody had ever gotten a device from patent to ready-to-market within a year. They had never seen anything like it, but we got turned down.

And that was fucking it.

I was broke, and I had to give up my car (I couldn't keep my rent and my car).

I thought, what the fuck am I going to do next?

Well, that's about the time that Uber came to town.

I went to one of those cheapie lots, and told them I didn't have any credit. I asked if I could buy a car and they said yeah. I bought a little Nissan and started driving Uber. In nine months, I had 47,000 miles on it, and I was making $900 a week. For six months, I was the only daytime driver in Gainesville (Uber was promoting the need for nighttime drivers for college kids). Then I traded it in for a new Honda Civic and logged another 37,000 miles.

After two years, a 4.9 rating, more than 7,200 rides, I made more than $70,000.

I got back on my feet financially.

Driving Uber and being a weed consumer (I never smoked in the car, but I always smelled like weed), I met lots of people.

Many of them would get in and sniff sniff sniff.

Then they'd smile.

"Mmmmmmmm."

The entrepreneur in me had an idea.

"This might be a good place to start back in the weed business."

CHAPTER 21

BACK IN BUSINESS

When I started Uber in July 2015, I basically stayed at my house and picked up rides as I wanted them. That is, until some of the fuckers who were just starting out figured that I was basically getting a lot of rides, so they hovered around my house picking up rides that should have been mine. I felt like killing some of those fuckers. I eventually got out because my PTSD got the better of me.

While Uber got me back on my feet financially, it did something else much bigger: It put me in touch with so many people. Everyone, it seemed, wanted weed.

I've never seen a place like Gainesville. It's a small college town in north central Florida, not near anything. Couple hours from Tampa, Orlando, and Jacksonville. Farm towns around the outskirts. A big old university in the center of town with not much industry otherwise, except health care.

Gainesville folks wanted their weed. Damn, I'm sure there are other towns like this, but I haven't seen it.

The people I met in Uber ran the range—professors, doctors, loads of college students. Didn't matter who they were or what they did. They wanted to smoke.

Uber is how I started and expanded my network. At one point, I met the biggest weed dealer in town. He was a young guy, and he was selling so much weed that he decided to retire—in his 20s—and built a house in Colorado. Made a ton. That guy drove his motorcycle around town and was serving 75 people a day. He did it for four years, then retired. Fucking crazy. Gainesville is a small town by most standards, but it was big when it came to marijuana.

Now, it took me a while to learn how it all worked. I didn't get a good Gainesville connection for weed until 2013 or so. For years before that, I was still driving south to St. Pete every three weeks to pick up a quarter pound of weed for myself. Eventually, I did meet a connection—a guy who would deliver me really high-quality weed for a decent price. I wanted the good stuff. For a long time in Gainesville, all that was available was mid-quality—not horrible, but not great.

With Uber, I had my local sourcing to get my pot, but now the plan was to expand. If my Uber conversations turned to weed, that was a good thing. We'd chat, connect, then some of them would come by the house, and we'd just shoot the shit about pot. All this time, I was trying to find clients and suppliers for good stuff. And I was making some good friends along the way too.

Finally, maybe six months into my Uber gig, I met a guy named LoveBoy. He was a big player in the scene, and I wanted to start selling more—and get into the edible business. So I started working with LoveBoy.

LoveBoy, that fucker, taxed me hard on my prices—charging me way too much.

But that's how I got started in Gainesville. I'd buy a quarter-pound from him, turn it over, buy another quarter, turn it over, again and again. I'd do that about three days a week.

It wasn't hard after that. Once people find out you have weed, the fucking town blows up, and everybody wants some. Word-of-mouth is the best business tool we have. I'd always vet the people out. I didn't deal with any strangers. If you wanted weed, either I had to know you or you had to come by the house with someone I knew, so I could make sure you were ok.

I have a couple suppliers, but I still used LoveBoy until recently.

And fuck, that's just one guy in Gainesville. There are dozens more like that—all serving this small town.

I used several different suppliers until I met the one I finally wanted to use exclusively, because you're always meeting new people, and you're always searching for better prices and better quality. So much of it is shit quality, and I demanded good weed, because people deserve to have good flowers. I mean, these college kids, they're smoking bad shit half the time, and they don't even know what they're missing. So when you get them good weed, that's the game-changer. They want your weed, and they want a good high at a decent price without having to smoke a shit-ton of it. And that's not even mentioning all the bad shit that's going on with fentanyl. So trust is a big part of this business; people need to know they're getting high-quality—and safe—drugs.

In 2018, a guy moved in close by to me, and I was talking to him in the neighborhood.

"What do you do?"

"I'm in the candy business," I said, and I brought him in and showed him my store of edibles that I was making.

The next day, he knocked on my door, and he showed me a pound of beautiful weed.

"Can you do anything with this? My friend sent it to me."

"Fuck yeah!" I said.

The price was exceptional, so I paid him cash right on the spot.

"I can get some more," he said. So he got four more pounds. This was northern California weed, which was great, because it pushed LoveBoy to give me better weed (and at better prices).

That did come with some pressure, because not only do you have to get the weed across the country, you have to get the cash back there too. And that wasn't easy. Same shit—people stealing the money from the packages that we sent. These West Coast suppliers liked it—because they wanted an East Coast outlet. That's because there's so much weed out west that you can't make much money because it's so pervasive out there. But if they can get a contact in the East Coast, they can charge more and make more. So they loved dealing with me.

Finally, I had enough of dealing with the headaches of getting the pot from out west and sending the cash back (it got to the point where I had to send people out with the cash to make sure it was safe). So I just started dealing with local suppliers—a couple college guys.

In the beginning, I was starting with my quarter-pound, but it grew and grew and grew. Over time, you build up trust and credibility, and my prices were getting better because of the competition between my West Cast supplier and LoveBoy. So I had established a good business though I do have to admit the prices have become crazy. I was paying $15 a pound when I did the Colombia smuggles, and now these fuckers were charging upwards of $2,000 a pound. That's wrong. But fuck, as long as everybody's smoking, it doesn't matter.

By 2017, I had a phenomenal customer base through Uber. I'd deliver weed to people, they'd come over to the house, all was good. At one point, I was doing Uber a lot, and I couldn't keep up with all my weed contacts, so I handed off my contact list to the Colorado Kid. But when he retired, all of his clients were wondering what the fuck they were going to do.

And that got me back.

It wasn't hard to build back up, because they knew me. Once you establish yourself with a good reputation and reliable medicine, people will keep coming back and coming back. Hell, some of these college kids, when they come back into town after summer or something, I'm the first person they call.

"Can I stop by?" they ask.

Hell yes.

"God we missed you!" they'll say.

In 2017, in Colorado, the pot market was about 55 percent in edibles. That's in a legal state. I saw the future, and I saw the numbers. And I knew that was the direction to take the business.

Fuck, this is what I needed to start. If the market is that high this soon, it was sure to grow and be a lucrative path for business.

Anybody could sell weed, I figured, but let's see what we can do with the edibles.

Now, I'd always been into edibles for my own. I had always liked making pot brownies—sending them to my sister and daughter. And

I just started reading and researching. Reading and researching. Reading and researching.

And I learned as much as could about the process of extraction and making edibles. I bought the equipment and engineered my first press.

When we used to get a boatload of Jamaican weed, there was always a case of over-proofed rum—a Jamaican rum (151 proof) stuffed with blue mountain buds. It came in these bottles and the liquid turned dark green with so much resin from the THC that broke down in the rum. It would coat your throat with hash oil. You couldn't drink it straight because it was so strong and harsh. It was the strongest goddamn alcohol you ever had. You have just a little bit in a glass with a little Coke and you'd be on the couch for the rest of the fucking night—and probably the next day too.

Knowing that was helpful when I learned to squeeze the plants, extract the THC, and have these patties left over. And I don't fucking like wasting cannabis, and I could see there was still some THC left in the patty. How the fuck am I going to get it out?

Ah, over-proofed rum will get it out.

Fuck, I couldn't find any around here, so I bought grain alcohol—180 proof. I'd fill up a jar with the alcohol and the patties and let it sit. And I started making a tincture—the grain and the THC. I'm not drinking, mind you, but I got customers who wanted it—little jars, droppers, and misters. People didn't like the fucking taste but it was a great pain medicine. I did that for a little bit.

The business now is mostly desserts, like lollipops, cookies, gummies. I even make a butter and did some THC hot sauce. People love the edibles, of course.

I've handed most of my recreational clients off to others, and now most of the people I serve are using for medicinal purposes. They just want to fucking sleep or get rid of some pain or feel better. I even have local doctors who tell their patients to see me when their patients are tired of the fucking Big Pharma meds being pumped into their bodies and not doing a damn thing to help.

Now, I've handed off a lot of my business to others to do the selling. I have one beautiful college girl who makes a killing. She dresses all sexy and sells joints to the frat boys. Smart fucking marketing if you ask me. Weed with a side of wow. One time, she stopped by, had her bikini on, and told me she was going to sell joints up and down the beach. She just loves the business. Real smart girl. I've also got a few others who sell, and I have a lady friend who does a lot of my cooking.

Nowadays, there are new students who come to the University of Florida for the first time, and they already know about "the old man in town," because they've already talked to other friends in town.

I've handed off customer lists of a hundred people three different times, and I still have a couple hundred people I work with. It just never ends. The demand is always there.

It's just one constant loop:

Anybody who has good weed smokes it and shares it with their friends, and the friends say, "Where do I get some of that?"

That's the way it expands. I get my weed into the hands of people who can get it into the hands of other people.

I had read the science, and I knew how important good weed was.

Since 2015, I've gone through about a thousand customers. They come, they go, they graduate, they move.

It's just taken on a life of its own that I just can't shut off. Some weeks I work seven days a week making candy and meeting with my customers (and meeting the new ones that they bring over).

I'm now looking into entheogens and mushrooms because this is also part of our medicinal future—so much more so than weed because Big Pharma is researching the fuck out of this because they are in tune to the healing and calming power of entheogens. Many of my customers have overcome serious childhood trauma, depression, and anxiety by eating them. It's been amazing, really. And it's the next frontier in pain management and mental health, I truly believe.

The majority of my customer base likes me not just for my products, but for my knowledge and opinion and my help with their problems. In a lot of ways, I'm a counselor to them too. I have a tribe of great people. I'm their tribal medicine man. Natural medicine.

Here's the way I look at things: This is a service business for me. I could make a lot more money than I do and more than I have, because the market demand is high. But I actually cut my prices when the economy is bad to help people when they most need it.

I've come to the conclusion that anybody who has been in the service and served honorably has had it engrained in them that service is part of their DNA.

People often ask me if I'm worried about getting caught or getting busted.

Nah. It's only jail!!

It would cost them so much to jail me—just in my heart medicine alone—that it's not worth it for them. And here in Gainesville, they've really stopped busting people for pot. Or they don't care. I'm an old man, so it doesn't make any sense for them to do anything to me at this stage in my life. But you never know.

CHAPTER 22

WHAT'S COOKING

I look back and I think back at how everything I did converged to this path. My skills in engineering with rocketry made it easy for me to learn the mechanics of pressing and making edibles. My skills I learned in crime made it easy for me to relate to people (not to mention understanding business skills and entrepreneurship). My journey as an alcoholic taught me about the human spirt and the sense of giving to other people. My education in physical therapy informed my views on healing, people, pain—and the intense back-asswards ways that our pharmaceutical systems worked. And my relationships along the way—with my sisters, my mom, my grandmom, my kids, my love interests, my clients, my enemies, my allies—really helped me understand all the nuances and emotions of what it fucking means to be a human and dealing with all of life's fucked-up shit.

Above all, as I stand here today, I know that I'm doing something that makes a difference in people's lives. In a very real way. In a very tangible way. And in a very meaningful way.

With marijuana, I help a lot of people deal with their physical and emotion pain.

I get thanked every fucking day.

Bottom line: Marijuana is a basic commodity that every human should be able to grow in their own yard and have when they want. Because they can't, people like me have to come along to help take care of them.

As long as you don't rip people off or fuck them over in the marijuana business, all is good. My introduction was with Jamaican weed, and I learned a lot about the Rastafarian movement and the spiritual aspects associated with it.

From the very beginning for me, cannabis has been a very spiritual experience. (Kids today are introduced to it through pop-culture Cheech and Chong idiotic ways.)

While there are medicinal benefits to smoking marijuana and doing mushrooms, the bigger effect is spiritual.

You expand your mind beyond the boundaries that have been set by school and church and all the other rule-makers in our lives. And you realize your mind is so much more capable than you ever dreamed of. That's what it's always been about for me. When you're locked into one ideology your whole life but then you start learning about the world, your mind opens up in whole new ways.

For me, it's about spirituality and healthcare. It's why I created T-shirts that say, "You can't spell Healthcare without THC."

And I remember the people that the products have helped. Taking the pain away from people suffering from cancer. Taking the edge off for people who have lived with anxiety medications. Helping people sleep. Helping people relax. Helping people open their minds.

Helping people heal.

Thousands of years ago, hashish was used as part of Hindu ceremonies, and I've always seen my weed journey as part of the spiritual journey and an intellectual one, as well as the medicinal one.

So yeah, when I think about all the people whose lives get better because they smoke weed or eat a lollipop, I get fucking livid about the way the government has treated marijuana. Yes, laws are changing, and I foresee a day when marijuana is legal across the board. But when I look back on my life—on my adventures, my smuggle to and from Colombia, my jail time, my cocaine party days, my loves and my losses—I do think back on this war on drugs.

I think about the people whose lives are immeasurably improved with better sleep, less pain, and more highs.

So yeah, I stand by the four words I said on the dock that night when I got back from my first Colombian smuggle. Fuck you, Richard Nixon.

LIFE LESSONS FROM THE WORLD OF WEED

When you've lived the life I have over the last 76 years, you see a lot, you do a lot, you live a lot, and you learn a lot.

The drugs. The smuggling. Loves and losses. New jobs, new adventures, new challenges.

I still learn something new every day. That's one of my joys in life—learning, thinking, and talking with all of the people who come through my business.

I agree with the philosopher who said that the biggest thief in the world is the person who has knowledge and doesn't share it. That's one of the reasons why I love what I do. I love talking to people, teaching them about marijuana and mushrooms, and counseling them about the major lessons in life that I've gained through all of my experiences. You should do the same: Pass along what you know to those around you.

I look back on my life and all the things I've done over the years, and I think everything I have done and experienced comes together — what I do in my house every day in terms of making products, dispensing knowledge, and easing pains.

I've shared some of those lessons directly and indirectly throughout this book, but I also wanted a place where I could synthesize some of my thoughts (and tell you about some other experiences I've had)—to pass along what I've learned in this world to those who are open to hear it. Here are a few of the things that have really stuck with me—and I hope are, in some way, helpful to you too.

Trust is one of our most powerful tools.

Once I made the decision to go into cannabis business, it was all new to me. I had to learn it. I had to rely on other people. I had to absorb a lot of new information. I had to take risks. I had to fucking face consequences for my actions. It was a whole educational experience for everyone. How do you know who to trust and how do you develop that sense? Fuck, I don't have a specific formula, but I have a lot of thoughts on what trust means and how you can think about using it in your own life, or at least it's how I try to teach people about it.

Bonding builds trust. Way back when I started, I didn't just pick up guys off the street to work with me. How could I trust people to smuggle? I worked with people who I got high as fuck with. We partied, we drank, we smoked, and yeah, you share some serious shit and go through things together when you do that. That's what helps you build trust over time—by having shared experiences together. It's one way to earn it. And I would also argue that doing drugs improves your ability to expand your mind—and that's a key to knowing who to trust. A lot of people freak out on drugs, but I could trust the people who didn't freak out because I trusted the way their minds worked.

Want me to trust you? Meet my standards. Anybody who didn't respect my standards automatically got my distrust. Don't do the things I need you to do and you're out. Fuck, I'm dealing with a lot of serious stuff—as a smuggler, as a first mate and captain on a fishing boat—so you need to do things the right way. And I don't apologize for that. Now, I will say that the only way you got real trust in the drug business was to do jail time—and never give anyone up. That's the way people know they can really trust you—that you won't say anything about them when you could.

Quick story: When I was first mate on a boat, I'd have to teach all the new guys everything we did. "Teach 'em how to fish, Gary," the captain would say. And I got six new guys who didn't know shit. When you're out in the middle of the Atlantic, you have to set standards or people fucking die. I would set them all up in a group and teach them how to tie knots, set up the gear, cut bait, bait their hooks, and all that shit. I also told them that once we got off-shore, I'd go around and work with each person individually to make sure they knew what they were doing.

"You've been all shown how to do the right thing," I'd tell them, "and if you don't do it right, your ass is mine."

They were afraid of me, as they should have been. I wasn't mean. I was firm.

One trip, this kid went down into the engine room to do something. Up top, something didn't feel right so I went down to check. This fucking kid had turned the wrong valve and opened up one inadvertently, which started sinking the boat. Water is up to my knees in a 65-foot trawler. I'm yelling at him and I'm working to fucking find the right valve to shut it off. I pumped the water out.

When I came top side, I had a long screwdriver in my hand. I was going to stab that motherfucker and throw him overboard. He fucking almost killed me at sea, so I was going to kill him.

Captain told me he had locked the kid away so I couldn't get to him because he knew how pissed I was.

I told that kid to do the world a favor and never fish again. "You're too stupid. Go find something else to do," I said. And I fired him.

When we got back to the dock, he wanted to get paid. We started fighting right next to the sea wall. I'm beating the piss out of him, but I can't knock him out. In a sudden move, he jumped up and shouldered me—and I went over the edge. I caught myself, and when I got back on the deck, I saw him high-tailing it down the street. Never saw him again.

I have strong survival skills because of the situations I've been in, but the point is that trust comes from having high standards—and meeting them.

Trust is about trusting yourself first. Trust is a people skill—knowing how to read people. I've always been good at it, and I've always trusted myself. Maybe it was overconfident or arrogant to think that, but I just trusted my gut when it comes down to people and know who you should or shouldn't trust. Having lived the life I've lived, I got pretty good at it all. If your gut doesn't tell you something is right, it probably isn't. Trust your gut.

We need more collective courage.

Many people are ruled by fear: fear of getting caught, fear of getting in trouble, fear of what people think about them, fear, fear, fear. I've never been afraid—even captaining that boat into the thick of massive marijuana smuggle. Fuck, prison, to me, was just the cost of doing business. And I told myself that there were only two bad things that could happen to me—I could die at sea or I could go to jail. I wasn't afraid of jail (but I made sure I wasn't going to do any violence—no guns, no serious shit—no money or drugs are worth taking a human life), and I wasn't even afraid of dying. And once you realize that, you get a whole lot more freedom and power in your life.

Now, I can't tell you to flip a switch and automatically get courage. In a lot of ways, I do think, for the most part, you're either born with it or not. I happened to be born with it. Never did give a fuck. I always was ready for whatever consequences awaited me—jail, physical harm, all of it. I just never was scared of any of it. I used to get my ass beat all the time, and I laughed. Grandma used to take me out of church and shake me because I was being rowdy, and I just shrugged. Punishment just hurts for a minute. That being said, I'm not really a confrontational guy, so it's not like the movies where you see all these beat-him-up scenes between dealers and buyers (it was a much more peaceful time in the 1970s).

I've always lived by the mantra that sometimes the bear gets you, and sometimes you get the bear.

I've done hundreds of thousands of transactions. And have come out on top way more times than not. Fuck that bear.

So I ask you, what are you afraid of? And what are you not doing that you really want to?

Take the fucking step.

My dick might not work very well anymore, but I still got balls.

Most people we see every day are in a prison in their own making. The first time I was ever in jail—it was minimum-security—I saw first-hand how living in a totalitarian environment would be like. Company store, company rules, company food, company sleeping arrangements. We do what they say we're going to do.

Yeah, that's prison. But you know what? There are institutional prisons all around society that lock us into ideology and that lock us into ways of thinking that handcuff our freedoms and instinct as humans.

The big one that comes to mind: Religion. Religion can lock people into an ideology and consume people—and define who they are. We see this all the time. I saw it growing up in a family with a religion-obsessed father. He never learned to accept anything outside the orthodoxy. Another one: Politics. We accept one way of thinking, which puts us in a vulnerable position to believe everything that our leaders say, rather than thinking for ourselves and realizing that the world is a much more complex place than our politicians make it out to be. How about this one? The corporate workforce. Go to college, work at the same company for four decades and then retire. You're locked into that company's rules, systems, and ways of thinking—and you're basically unallowed to be *you*. Go into a factory every day, do the same thing for eight hours, and then clock out. That's a prison. That's a prison of freedom.

I've always taken that to heart. People have locked themselves in a certain—and radical—ideology, and anybody who disputes it is crazy.

How did all this happen? Basically, it's what we were taught by our parents (and what was taught to our parents by their parents and so on). We accepted it as a way of life rather than thinking openly and critically for ourselves.

So here's the interesting thing. Prison—the kind I served in—is actually a lot different than the ideological prison many people live in. Sure, they can take your body and put it in a cell. They can take your time and lock you up for whatever your sentence is.

But they can *never* take your mind.

They can *never* stop your brain from working.

My kind of prison actually gives people a chance to change their mind, reset their thinking, recalibrate their lives, get a different perspective on life. Fuck, I read thousands of books in my three total years in prison—what the fuck else am I going to do? You don't think that opened my mind to all different parts of the world and all different ways of thinking? Fuck yeah it did. In fact, the last time I was in prison, I did some serious thinking—that if I didn't change my ways or my life, I'd be spending the majority of my life locked up. And I didn't want that, so I did change. And that's what got me on the right track—to go to college, to study physical therapy, to change the way I lived. I had to open my mind to that after years and years of living the drug-smuggling, drug-doing, booze-filled life. (I should say that yeah, nobody wants to be in prison, but in my experience, most of the people in physical prison are there because of some self-inflicted problem, like alcohol. That's a prison too.)

Take the physical prison out of the equation and go back to the mental one: These people who are locked into my-way-only type of thinking? Fuck. That's the real prison that's having a huge effect on the way our society is functioning (more like dysfunction).

155

True freedom is having an open mind.

An open mind to explore.

An open mind to make good choices that help people.

An open mind to challenge your ways of thinking.

An open mind to think for—and be—yourself.

That, of course, takes work. You have to want to be *open*.

For me, it always goes back to the AA Acceptance Prayer: Accept the things you cannot change, change the things you can, and have the wisdom to know the difference.

That brings me peace, satisfaction, and serenity every day.

We're all just passing through.

One of my favorite cartoons as a hippie on the beach was this hairy old man with the caption "just passing through." Damn, if that's not one of my mottos that I live by. We're all just passing through this life, so we might as well as have a whole lot of fun while we're doing so.

Every hour fishing is another hour added to the end of your life.

Fishing is so peaceful and so much fun. Plus, it's something that just puts you so close to Mother Nature—one of the true spiritual experiences in life.

My fishing life started with my grandpa—fishing every weekend at the lake. Go out at sun up, fish until sun down, catch our limit, and go back and do it again. I learned hard lessons in those days—when I cast and knotted my line, I had to untangle every fucking knot. He'd be fishing, and I'd be untangling. And that lesson stuck with me: You gotta do things the right way.

Fishing has always been part of my life, even before I tried to make a living at it. I fished back home in Indiana, I did it in Florida (first time I did it on a family trip, I won for the biggest fish—big fucking red groupers—and I loved it). One of my challenges early on in Florida was wanting to catch snook. They're amazing. They hit the line like a freight train, so you gotta be strong and you can't let them run. Ferocious fucking fish. A beautiful fighting fish. Good to eat too.

When I turned to working on boats to learn the fishing industry, things got a lot more serious. When you're off-shore, you have to learn patience and you have to learn skills. And you must live in the present. It can be life and death out there, so you're not worrying about anything else in your life—you're doing what you needed to do to survive. That's *living*. Be in the moment. You can't control anything what happened 10 minutes before that moment, and you can't predict anything that's going to happen 10 minutes from now. But you can control what you can control in the NOW. And that has been one of my driving mantras in life.

All my senses were fully alive when I was off-shore. (Land was much more challenging to me—wine, women, and weed.) Being off-shore for two weeks at a time was all about survival instinct. You have to respond to your environment, and I think that understanding Mother Nature has been the most important thing in my life—seeing it calm and seeing it violent, damn. That teaches you respect, that brings life into focus, that brings you a clarity that few other things can do. And that's when I felt most alive.

(I'm now on a plant-based diet, so I've changed my approach to killing fish and animals, but I am appreciative of what I learned and experienced along the way.)

Know your weaknesses and confront them.
Life is so much easier with no alcohol. Following the 12 steps of AA gave me a spiritual foundation and understanding to change my life.

Stop chasing.
I used to chase life. I used to push that rock up a hill—with dreams of success, with dreams of doing more, with always wanting to get the next thing. I stopped pushing the rock up the hill. I started letting life come to me. There's natural energy that's drawn to me because of what I do and who I am. And that, I've found, is not only a new me—but also a new and better perspective on life now.

I sort of understand what life is—living in the moment and not trying to chase the next one.

There are so many damn benefits to marijuana.
I've been really encouraged by the relatively recent emphasis on the health aspects of cannabis, and not just the party aspects. I hate the pop culture aspect of weed (like Cheech and Chong), and I hate that's what gives cannabis a bad reputation. Living in Amsterdam made me realize how it should be normalized—just part of the culture, not blowing it out of proportion in pop culture (which the young kids see and then want to emulate in the dumb party culture).

All of that garbage clouds the perception of what the plant can do. Most intellectuals know that pot should never have been illegal because of its benefits. (We do have to guard against the fucked-up drugs—the stuff laced with fentanyl.) That's what gives drugs a bad name, the bad players. There's an extraordinary amount of the bad stuff coming into this country. It's one of the reasons why people are going to dispensaries—to get the clean stuff.) As I see it, weed has so many benefits. The main ones for me:

It expands your mind. And it gives you freedom to choose. I wasn't smoking to explicitly try to get fucked up (I had booze for that for so many years). For me, it was about being with people, expanding my mind, and learning so much more about life.

The health benefits. Cannabis has proven benefits in pain relief, anxiety, depression, stress relief, sleep assistance and so much more, and that's a big reason why so many people do it. I've helped cancer patients, MS patients, crazy people, you name it. The active ingredient of THC has done wonders. Fuck, there's a reason why the cannabis plant is on this earth, and I believe it's because of the medical benefits. The plant is all over the world. And if we could ever stand up to Big Pharma, the world would better embrace marijuana as medicine. I also firmly believe that weed cures and prevents Covid-19 (I got kicked off Facebook for saying so). But Canadian studies support this—that cannabis coats the layer of your cells to protect you. I haven't had Covid and I smoke a lot (and I came in contact with a lot of people, even during the height of the pandemic, so I was at high risk of contracting it).

Smoking weed (and all of its relatives) is a spiritual experience. Religion has been using the spiritual enlightenment of cannabis forever, and I've always grounded myself in the act that gave me a whole different perspective. Yeah, people do pot to get fucked up, but I do it to enhance my spiritual beliefs—getting closer to nature (to me, Mother Nature is my God). It keeps me grounded!

You don't fuck people.

Most of today's dealers fuck their customers on things like weight, quantity, or price. And that's what also gives drugs a bad name, because the whole industry is premised on the fact that bad people are going to do bad things to make more money (sounds a lot like corporate America huh?). Well, I've always tried to live by the mantra that you just don't fuck people. I charge people what the product is worth and what the market is willing to bear based on the quality. That's the way an upstanding business should work. You treat people right, and you deliver what's best for them. Not a bad way to live no matter what kind of work you do, ay?

It took me a while to learn this, and I attribute it to getting sober. Once I got sober, I developed a conscious and started to realize that you just don't treat people badly. Because it sucks to live that way.

Speaking of fucking people…

Couple things I know to be true…

- Sex is not love.
- But I love sex. From day one, finding a relationship was getting with girls, because that's what us boys cared about.
- Lust is natural, and we shouldn't apologize for it. Passion is good.
- A good education in love and sex can make relationships better (and so few of us are exposed to it as kids). I never saw my parents in a loving relationship, and I'm sure that had some influence on how I approached my relationships and why many of them had problems. I had a mom and dad, but I didn't know what love was (we got our sex ed from Playboy magazine, and we got in trouble for those), besides natural

familial love. I never even got married to my first wife for love—it was all about convenience and getting off the military base.

- I took to heart advice that a friend who I met through AA gave me, telling me I tried fucking too many women, rather than getting to really know them. "You need to learn to like a woman without wanting to fuck her," he told me. And I took to that. I had never even considered it, but it was a real life lesson for me. I've learned. I've matured. I've appreciated the difference between fucking and loving and everything in between.

Try, fail, try, fail. And do it again and again.
That's life. But I never quit trying. I get up every day, thinking, what are we going to do today?

Entrepreneurism gives you freedom.
I couldn't see myself working for the same company doing the same job over and over for 30 or 40 years. I wanted to be outside. I wanted to control my life. I wanted the freedom to move when I wanted. I wanted to capitalize on my skill of seeing a need and trying to fulfill that need. And being an entrepreneur gives me freedom and independence. I don't have to take shit from anyone else. It doesn't work like that in any other industry. You have to take shit from other people. I don't. I sign the checks.

My philosophy: I give it my best shot and if it doesn't work out, that's ok (I have the same philosophy for my wives as I do for my businesses).

My first criminal enterprise was selling illegal fireworks in Indiana after getting them over the line in Missouri. People wanted them, and I figured out the way to supply them. That enterprise stopped when a whole box of fireworks in the back of my car started popping off after I threw a cigarette out the window. But I learned a lot in all of my entrepreneurial adventures.

Entrepreneurship is all about a supply issue and a need issue—and then you fill the gap.

I had no idea my current business in edibles would evolve the way it did. You have to give the people what they want—they're going to find it anyway, so why not me? And that's been a theme and a thread throughout my whole life. Why not me?

Not a bad phrase to say to yourself when you're wrestling with taking a leap into a new opportunity. (This especially came to light in the economic downturn of 2008 when people my age were laid off and didn't have opportunities. It became a necessity to go out on your own and try to be successful in entrepreneurial ways.)

The best part about working for yourself? I can use all of my skills in these kinds of ventures. My whole life's work all comes together—people skills, healing skills, business kills. I can do what I like—not what somebody else wants me to do.

Now, you don't have success without failures along the way. But really the key is that you have to be successful living life before you're successful in business. I get my satisfaction by helping people. I help a lot of people every day get through their pain, and that's what makes me truly happy.

We have it backwards when it comes to pain management.
In a lot of ways, you could argue that much of my life has centered around the pain business—or the pain relief business, that is. You could certainly say it during my physical therapist days, and you can absolutely say it when it comes to my life in drugs. I peddle in medicine. And I see the pain that people live in every day. Some serious physical pain. Some serious mental anguish. And I see first-hand how weed and mushrooms *work*. Natural, effective, without all the crazy prices of products produced by Big Pharma.

There are modalities used in Europe—that I learned in Europe—that are used to treat chronic pain effectively. As in, it's used one or two times and that's it—the pain is gone.

Take a guess as why we haven't adopted them.

Because if we had effective cures to chronic pain, how the fuck would Big Pharma make its money?

One example: A device that uses electrical currents to stimulate nerves through the spine—put the device on the part of the spine that's causing pain and in 20 minutes, that pain may never come back. I've seen it.

These things work. They stop chronic pain.

And the FDA wouldn't approve these kinds of modalities because the pharmaceutical industry wants to sell pain pills to the country.

That's fucking cruel.

When there's technology that can stop pain, why aren't we using it? I've used a procedure called deep-tissue laser therapy, which uses photobiomodulation to heal by penetrating to the bone and speeding up the healing process. At the time I saw a demo of it, I couldn't use my thumbs after a series of injuries. I couldn't tie my shoes, couldn't do shit, and I never dealt with it. At the demo, I was working in that mobile physical therapy unit. After five minutes on each hand, the pain was completely gone.

"That might last a couple hours, maybe 24 hours, it'll come back," the woman who did the treatment on me said. "But if you do it six times over a two-week period, that pain will never came back."

I followed the plan, and the pain never came back.

Holy fuck.

So we used the device in experimental mode on patients who saw us in the mobile unit (we did it for free for a while and eventually people had to pay out-of-pocket because it wasn't approved and wouldn't be covered by insurance).

I used it on one patient with diabetic neuropathy who had no feeling in her feet. I did one treatment and she started crying.

She hadn't felt the carpet on her feet in 12 years, and now she could.

Holy fuck.

Eventually, we had ladies coming out who wanted the treatment on their whole bodies. I was amazed at the results, but it never got approved.

Everything is driven by greed.

That's wrong.

And that's a huge reason why weed and mushrooms—huge healing agents—are so controversial. What if, by god, they eliminated the need for pharmaceuticals? That would threaten the big business of corporate America. Nobody is being honest. We deserve honesty.

It's not like people didn't know the power of marijuana. In 1937, the U.S. government made all drugs illegal. Up until then, a lot of research was going into cannabis. But then jazz music came out and the roaring '20s happened. White girls started going out, listening to jazz, and hanging out. And then the government couldn't have white women fucking black men (they thought of it in much more disparaging terms). So let's ban drugs!

Well now look at us.

We're in a world where people are full of pain, and there are methods that can help and heal.

I see it every day.

For me, marijuana and mushrooms are a spiritual thing.

But in many ways, they're a medical thing—because they work to help ease people's pain and mental anguish.

In fact, clients tell me all the time that my edibles aren't food. They're fucking medicine.

My motto has been all about healthcare.

Because it fucking works.

Weed is an illegal substance, but it shouldn't be.

Because it makes people better.

Religion is in the eyes and heart of the beholder.

I spent my whole life outside—hunting and fishing when I was a kid (fishing sucks, catching is great), spending months at a time at sea, water skiing on lakes, living my days on the beach. And I just fucking love nature. So majestic. So powerful. So many moments when you say, holy shit, how is that even possible? I mean, can you even wrap your head around the depth of the universe and how we're just a little fucking pinhead in it?

When I was in the belly of the storm out at sea during my Colombian smuggle, that's when it really hit me (and when I really felt like a little pinhead when the waves were eating us up like a snack): Mother Nature threw her best at me, and I survived. Not that I'd ever want to do that again, but wow, was that a powerful lesson in the glory of nature—and how we're all just a small piece of it.

So in a lot of ways, nature has been my religion. It's been a spiritual backdrop for me—granted, in less formal ways than organized religion, because God knows that I had quite the experience with organized religion growing up. You already know about that. I was forced into religion and the church by my father and family. We went to church all the time, but I always rejected Christianity. I didn't understand it, and nobody fucking explained a word of it. I never understood what the readings, the sermons, or the traditions meant—and how they related to me. You just accepted that "this is the way it is" because someone fucking told you to. Well fuck that. That's why I rejected organized religion from day one.

Things changed a bit for me when I started doing business in Rochester, New York. There, I met a group of people who organized themselves around Hinduism and Indian philosophy. (In college, when I took philosophy class, I realized how fucked up religion really was in that there are so many religions and so many beliefs, which opened my mind, but sure did make it all a lot more confusing.) So when I met these people, they explained to me that Hinduism is the mother of all religions—and that if you understood that, you could understand it all. Christianity didn't make any sense to me, but when I started doing Hindu readings, it did. It had existed thousands of years (and they used cannabis in their religious ceremonies, so that's surely had credibility with me), and those teachings and readings, I think, did help make me a better person.

Now, mind you, I was a raging alcoholic for most of my young-adult life, so organized religion was never something that I engaged in, and I didn't think of it in that sort of guiding-light kind of way.

But when I entered Alcoholics Anonymous, we started reading the book, Sermon on the Mount—the Key to Success in Life. Being in AA and reading that book saved my life. That book—I tell you—gave me an understanding of Jesus that I had never heard before. All of the Hindus I knew actually ridiculed Americans for not following the teaching of Jesus because he was the greatest teacher of all (I had always told them that I never fucking understood what they were fucking trying to teach me). When I finished that book, I cried and I cried. Because I finally got it.

All my life, I've felt like there's been a little angel on my shoulder protecting me—back in that storm, being in the middle of drug wars. Now, I got what I deserved at the time—jail time, more fights than I can count. But I still feel like I've been protected—and I've been able to follow my true bliss throughout life. All of my past roads have led me perfectly to this road I'm on now. I can only play the cards I've been dealt, and these are the cards I've dealt.

When I went back to school in Amsterdam when I was in my 50s (and all my peers were in their 20s), we had to fill out a little bio form about stuff we liked. In my form, I said my favorite movie was Pulp Fiction. I said my favorite book was Sermon on the Mount—The Key to Success in Life by Emmitt Fox.

One Jewish kid (they were all kids to me) said, "I read your bio and I asked my parents about Sermon on the Mount, and they said, 'This guy is alright.'"

And that sure is the way I feel. I'm fucking alright. With all of it.

I am not unsatisfied about any part of my life. No, I'm not proud of all of the decisions I've made and the things I've done. But I don't beat myself up over them. I treat people well. I help them heal. I've learned a lot—and I hope—taught a lot.

I run my life now through one basic philosophy that has served me well for many, many years: I have no control over yesterday, and I have no control over tomorrow. What I can control is what happens right now in this very moment—and be the best person I can be.

When it all comes to an end, I'll be with the earth

I'm going to be buried in a natural cemetery—they wrap you up in cloth and bury you in nature. That's the greatest spiritual thing you can do. I just want to keep it natural.

I'll be in the woods. And if anybody wants to come out and visit, they can come out and smoke a joint on my burial site.

I want marijuana free to anyone who wants it.

The government's war on weed has been one of the most egregious fucking things I've seen in my life. Weed is natural, it's a healing agent, and it works to help people. But the government ran scared—scared of Big Pharma, mostly, but also because of religion and race. And it's been a disservice to all the people who could benefit from weed. It's even scarier now because of all these drug dealers selling lousy shit and lacing it with fentanyl, so it's become a dangerous and bad business. (Which also speaks to the point why people come to me—they trust me.)

Do I see a future where weed is legally and readily available to anyone who needs it?

Yes, I see a day when we'll have people growing their own in their garden and using it as they need—pure, effective, medicinal. (And always remember, you can't uneat edibles. Start slowly.) The science supports the medical and mental benefits of marijuana and mushrooms, and I see a day when it can be sold widespread for those who can't grow it; taxes will be an alluring benefit for the government.

That would be the dream. Available to everyone: Give people what they want.

Help them heal. Help them live. Help them live the freedom that we all deserve.

ACKNOWLEDGEMENTS

I've lived a life of smuggling, of partying, of smoking, of learning, of loving, of so many things. And I'm grateful for all the family, friends, and business partners—most of whom are portrayed throughout the book—for being part of my journey.

I've always known I had a book in me (not many people have eluded the Coast Guard to bring several tons of weed from Colombia the way I did), and I'm thankful for everyone who helped me tell my story. Thank you to the team at Palmetto Publishing for publishing The Man at the Table. I'd also like to acknowledge Ted Spiker for his incredible help in writing this book, Stacston Carter for the cover art, and Mo'ney Roseman for website design.

Most of all, I've had the great pleasure of sitting across the table with thousands of different people. I'm grateful for every conversation, every transaction, and every connection that I've made. I hope I've brought as much pleasure to your life as you have to mine.

Milton Keynes UK
Ingram Content Group UK Ltd.
UKHW020820211123
432955UK00010B/39/J